MAKING

CHILDREN'S PARTIES

CLICK

MAKING

HARRISBURG, PENNSYLVANIA

CHILDREN'S

PARTIES

CLICK

by Virginia W. Musselman

 STACKPOLE BOOKS

To

HELEN DAUNCEY

Longtime and treasured friend

This book is dedicated

with affection

Contents

CREDITS

The ideas and suggestions in this book have come from personal experience and observation, and from friends and co-workers over many years. I wish that I could thank them all in person.

Special thanks for generous sharing of ideas should go to the recreation departments of Anchorage, Alaska and Sunnyvale, California. Our exchange of ideas over the years has been a pleasure to me.

My very special thanks go to my friend, Mary B. Cummings, for her help in meeting deadlines. I am deeply grateful to her.

Thanks also should go to the Girl Scouts of the U.S.A. for several recipes, and to the Florida Citrus Commission for its novel ideas for turning fruit into favors.

If I have failed to credit anyone for specific material, it has been inadvertent, and non-intentional, and I apologize.

A Word about Parties . . .

A party for children is very different from a party for teen-agers, or for adults. The major difference is the degree of *focus*.

In a teen-ager party, the spotlight may switch from the host or hostess to the most popular girl or boy present, or to the record album of the current objects of teen-age adulation, or to the party theme, location, or food. The young host or hostess brings the group together, but the group chooses its own focus.

In the successful adult party, there is an even greater sharing of attention. The host and hostess *try* to focus the spotlight of attention on the guests, to give them opportunities to be the center of discussions, to display their talents, exert their charms, and to meet and make new friends.

In a child's party, the focus is sharply upon that child. It is not shared. Everyone, including all adults involved, understands and accepts this. The child is the Big Chief, the King or Queen-of-the-Day. He or she is the undisputed center of interest, and accepts the spotlight with complete complacency.

These changes in point of view and in behavior are part of the maturing process, part of personality development. Emphasis on self gives way gradually to emphasis on others. Individual importance yields to social group relationships.

And here is the real reason why parties are important in the lives of children. They provide the setting in which children can (1) learn to accept and enjoy others, (2) find out that it can be pleasant to give as well as to accept attention and gifts, and (3) discover that sharing toys and taking turns can be fun. In the party setting they learn to talk easily with each other and with the adults present. They learn simple party manners. They develop social awareness.

In other words, it takes time—and opportunities—to learn to be generous, warm and outgoing instead of self-centered and demanding. The most remembered lessons are the ones that are learned through pleasant experiences. Parties provide such experiences. The child learns through play—and enjoys the lessons.

One more, less often mentioned reason why children's parties are important is that parents meet the young friends of their children, and by seeing them and their own in an informal, social setting, learn a great deal about both. How the child reacts to his party guests, or to being a guest at another child's party, can point out unexpected social gifts, or unsuspected gaps in his social maturity. His reactions can assist the parent in avoiding future overstimulation for the excitable child, or in providing additional opportunities for peer play for the over-timid child.

As far as the child himself is concerned, the whole idea of a party can be summed up in four words: Fun, Food, Favors, and ME. A party is his day in the sun—and he basks in it!

Quick Party-planning Guide

To find the just-right games and activities for each party or special occasion, use this alphabetical name index. It shows the usual good-time age level for each. Other special references, such as Safety, Favors, and the like, are also included, even though they may not have any specific age indication.

To save space, the following abbreviations have been used:

ALL—All Ages   so—Slightly Older (7–9)
vy—Very Young (4–6)   AT—Almost Teens (10–12)

Children have a way of falling out of adult-made classifications. Feel free to use your own judgment, and to select the activities that will make *your* party CLICK.

Alphabetical Listing	Good-Time Age Level				Page
	ALL	VY	SO	AT	
Cow's Eye		x	x		74–75
Crackerhead			x	x	75
Crazy Answers			x	x	98
Crocodile Race			x	x	73
Cup Dolls		x	x		63
Dash and Dot			x	x	63–64
Decorations					46–50
Ditch Him!			x	x	68
Dog and Bone		x			76
Dog and Rabbit			x		98
Doll Party		x	x		121–22
Donkey and Fiddler		x			105
Duck, Duck, Goose		x			76–77
Egg Animals	x				57
Egyptian Salute			x	x	75–76
Elephant			x	x	77–78
Farmer and the Crow			x		78
Favors					49–50
Feather Blow			x	x	85–86
Feed the Spider			x	x	99
Flying Saucers			x	x	58–59
Follow the Leader		x			78–79
Foo and Koo			x	x	103
Food Suggestions					39–45
Fortune-telling				x	48–49, 124–26
Fox and Squirrel			x		71
Frog Goggles		x			58
Frog in the Sea		x			71–72
Frog Race			x	x	79
Front Door Decor					46–47
Guest List, The					32–33
Ghost Trail		x	x		59
Goose Egg	x				106
Ha CHU, Ha CHO			x		106–07
Halloween Party	x				131–32
Halloween Safety					131
Hare and Tortoise Race		x	x		81
Hold Your Breath			x	x	107
Hot Potato			x	x	92–93
Hul Gul			x	x	99
Hunter		x	x		84
Husky Race			x	x	81

PART I

THE GLEAM-IN-THE-EYE PERIOD

or

"Don't Push the Party Panic Button!"

   The short chapters in this section are written to give you that why-not-try-it feeling about children's parties. They contain certain suggestions, comments, and safeguards that will make the party a pleasure instead of a problem.

Don't expect perfection. Don't expect children to act like perfect little ladies and gentlemen. (Come now! Do you know any perfect ladies and gentlemen?) Don't push them into maturity too soon. Childhood will never come again. Expect them to act like children. Help them to enjoy *being* children.

1

❧

What Makes Them Act That Way
or "I WON'T! I WON'T!"

Every adult who has ever lived through children's parties re-
members, with wry amusement, the times when a child's behavior
was completely baffling, when catastrophe was barely averted,
when tears flowed and screams rose above the party music. Who
could forget the party in which Elizabeth, charming in her new
party dress but overwhelmed by the attention, spent the entire
afternoon huddled in tears at the top of the stairs, refusing to
come down even for the cutting of her own birthday cake? Or the
time when Carol calmly announced: "I feel thick"—and *was*—all
over the newly upholstered chair? Or the afternoon when Dave
and George, left alone for a few minutes, emerged from the
waterlogged bathroom wet to the skin but smiling angelically
after an exhilarating water battle? Or the horrifying moment
when Peggie met Michael at the front door and declared firmly:
"You can't come to my party. I don't *like you*." Or Betty's
slumber party when she was twelve? How you woke up at three
A.M. and heard the record player still blaring out the favorite
record album. How you went down with fire in your eye—and
found all the girls snuggled in their sleeping bags, sound asleep.

Some of those party events are funny to look back on, but they
weren't always so funny while they were happening. A fight, even
a *little* fight, between two little boys—or girls—or both!—is not a

pleasant party activity. Tears are not happy-making. Minor accidents to furniture or china can frighten a child and annoy an adult. A skinned knee or scraped elbow can produce screams far out of proportion to the size of the child or the extent of the injury.

What makes them act like that? Perhaps it is because we expect too much, too soon. Perhaps it is because we provide too much, too fast. Perhaps the child and his party are just not age-compatible. The younger the child, the fewer the guests should be, and the shorter, more simple the party.

Even when following all the rules, don't expect every party to click. Most of them will, but some just won't. When that happens, keep your sense of humor and try again soon.

He's One!

The first birthday is a big day for parents, but not for Baby! He won't know what it is all about. He'll bask in the air of approval around him. He'll reach for the new rattle—and throw it overboard a few minutes later.

If friends and neighbors come in to celebrate Birthday # 1, make any other little ones comfortable, but plan for their proud parents. *They're* the ones who'll eat the birthday cake and enjoy a cup of coffee. Let the Birthday Boy or Girl be passed around for oh-ing and ah-ing, accept the gifts brought to him, take snapshots of him at his first party—and put him back in his crib for his nap!

The Tantrum-y Twos

The wise parent doesn't try to plan much more than a token party for the Twos. In the first place, they have to be watched every second. Everything is so new and exciting to a Two that he *must* touch, taste, smell and feel it. He's learned the pride of possession, also, and often refuses to share his toys, or games. Snatching, grabbing and screaming are common traits at two.

He plays so hard that he wears himself out and needs frequent quiet rest periods. He's concerned with what is in his immediate scope of understanding. Don't expect him to enjoy a long trip, or tall buildings, or a movie, or *anything* for a long period of time. He's too busy absorbing and cataloging the marvelous things around him to be much impressed with the world outside his home.

When planning a party for a Two, keep it very short, invite as few other children as you can without antagonizing your friends and neighbors—and expect the worst! There'll be toy-snatching, tears, and screams of anger, but the Twos can enjoy very simple singing games, will listen to a story, and will be delighted with cake and ice cream. They will very likely embarrass you with their frank comments on the gifts given them.

The Pleasing Threes

Threes have learned all about the child next door. They *like* people. They like to be liked. They have discovered that it is fun to be together, to play house, doctor and nurse, supermarket, airplane, and school. They like to go on little trips, to "dance" to music, to swing, ride a tricycle, build block houses. And they like to "dress up" for special occasions like parties. They are usually generous at this age, and enjoy giving as well as getting presents.

Food and favors are still the most important part of a party, but Three will enjoy anticipating it and talking about it later. Parties for Threes will be pleasant, if the guests are kept fairly few in number. If possible, include children that the little host knows and likes, for Three is growing up and learning to be selective. He is beginning to choose among people. He is developing likes and dislikes.

The Sunny Fours

Four has learned to enjoy a crowd, a *small* crowd of his friends. He enjoys making plans, taking trips to buy party food and favors, making presents. He loves playing the host. He's a giggler, a joker, a riddler. He asks questions, and *almost* listens to the answers.

He's bursting with life. Picnics and excursions are great fun, because Four is developing a sense of adventure. At Four, he still plays alongside of, rather than *with* other children. Games must be simple, dramatic, and involve motion.

Four can tolerate more playmates without getting upset. Parties for Four begin to have real meaning, and are increasingly important to his social development.

The Friendly Fives

Five is one of the nicest ages to be. Five begins to have his own opinions. "I like blue better than green." "I like chocolate better than vanilla." Five is a people-watcher. Nancy's mother hears her own words imitated as Nancy and Jean play dolls. Bob's father hears his opinion of a political figure or a make of automobile repeated solemnly by Bob as he talks to Dave while he and Dave are loading his wagon with blocks, or playing walkie-talkie.

Five has learned to run and jump, hop and skip, and he's working on whistling. He's not too good at following rules, but he likes games. In fact, Five likes almost everything, and he nearly always has a great time at a party. His snaggle-toothed grin is very appealing. His curiosity about the world around him makes him talkative and adventurous. Fives are fun.

Six and Up

Once the youngsters have started to school, new playmates, games, songs, and social activities become accepted, and parties assume a real importance. The boy and girl who have had the opportunity of being host and hostess at their parties will develop an increasing social awareness. Those children will find it easier, later on, to meet new people, carry on an interesting conversation, enjoy new activities and adjust to new situations.

These Six-to-Teens have one major characteristic: ENERGY.

Parties for them must have *action*. As they get closer to adolescence, the I-hate-boys and I-hate-girls phase can be handled by all-boy, or all-girl events, ranging from parties to picnics, sleep-ins to sleep-outs, trips to treasure hunts.

And as they reach the upper years before adolescence, they will very likely demand "grown-up" affairs, including music and dancing. Much of it will be mostly giggling, pushing, teasing, etc., but to them it means they're beyond "kid stuff." Picnics, beach parties, ski trips, boating, treasure and scavenger hunts, and other active and exciting events will give them a taste of the teens without making too many demands on them in the way of boy-girl relationships.

Actually, these groups enjoy games although they won't admit it. Games give them something to do with their hands and feet, and provide outlets for shrieking, giggling, and teasing. But don't *call* them games. Just start in, without any special names or explanations. Keep the action going, and they'll go along with it!

2

❧❧❧

The Parent Problem
or *"I Can Go by My SELF!"*

It sometimes comes as a delightful shock to a parent to hear a neighbor or friend say with real feeling, "Your Carol has such *nice* manners!" It's not so pleasant a shock for that parent to see Carol go into her most annoying "show-off" antics when she is taken visiting or to a party. Sooner or later every parent must accept the fact that the child away from home and parents is a different child—for a while anyway. And that goes for Bob, Anne, Bill and Susie—all the children that your child wants to invite to his party. Very frankly, the fewer the parents looking on, the easier the party will go.

Of course, with the Ones, Twos and even Threes, it doesn't much matter, because children that young don't really play *with* the other children. They'll just be there, and will enjoy new toys, attention, and a taste of ice cream, but the event is likely to be more of a Koffee Klatch for the parents than a real party for the children. The occasion will be short, with each mother keeping an eagle eye on her offspring, to see that he doesn't swallow a foreign object, pull the cloth off the table, or grab the cat by its tail. Child on lap or in sight, mother will enjoy the woman-talk over and above the sounds the children make.

When the children become Fours, Fives and Sixes, parents become party problems. In the first place, a youngster becomes self-conscious when parents are watching, or helping to direct, his play. He expects the mother of the young party-giver to be there. It's OK if his and other parents help to serve the food; that's what mothers are *for!* But the fewer parents the better!

In the first place, parents are so *big!* They take up so much room. The house has only so much space, and that space is needed for party games.

In the second place, parents often interfere. They just can't seem to help trying to improve things. "No, it's not your turn, David." "Carol, Bill touched it first." "Anne, put your shoe back on." "No, Barbara, it's not time to go home yet." They can make the youngsters—and *you*—self-conscious and defensive.

On the other hand, as the age level gets higher, the size of the party gets larger, and you'll need help—*parent* help. It's important, then, to work out some happy medium, and this will take planning ahead. It will also take your best party promotion and parent publicity.

The Child Who Is Too Young or Too Old

Frankness pays off. Mrs. B. down the street won't have her feelings hurt if you telephone and talk to her. Tell her about the party, that it's only for Fours and Fives, and that you know she'll agree that Dave is too young or too old for that group. If it is politic, ask her to let Davie come over at 4:30, to help eat the ice cream and cake. Be sure that Davie gets a Boodle Bag, too, if the others have favors to take home.

Often in a family there'll be several children with only a year or two difference in ages. Can you invite one without the other? If the party is for all-girls or all-boys, you can use that as a reason for inviting Bonnie but not Bob, and vice versa. If there'll be girls *and* boys, it's a good idea to try to keep the age range as close to two years' difference as possible. It won't always be possible. In fact, you'll want to break this general rule in the case of children who you know are very mature for their age. It *is* a good general rule, however.

It is also a good general rule to invite the same number of

guests as the host child has years. Here again, it just may not be possible. It can be worked out in many cases, however, by explaining to friends and neighbors, and by inviting some of the children who can't be kept out to come over for refreshments.

If the party is to be a trip party, then the size of the car or station wagon puts a legitimate limit to the number of guests. This is offset, however, by the fact that more adults are needed for trips—one for at least every eight guests for the eight-to-twelves, and more for the under-sevens.

Parent Pick-ups

A big problem, especially when children are invited who are too young to come alone, or to cross streets, is getting them there and then getting them back home. Parents may arrive too early, when you're busy putting the finishing touches on the decorations, or dressing the young host or hostess. Parents may arrive late, and linger too long, keeping you from getting the party started. Parents may be late in coming to pick the child up at the end of the party, and you'll have one or more tired, cross or overexcited youngsters to cope with, when you'd like to get the house straightened up before dinner.

The perfect solution, if you can possibly arrange it, is to provide transportation to and from the party. This relieves the parent from such annoyances as having to watch the clock or trying to find parking space; in fact, it can mean Mother's afternoon out, or a built-in baby-sitting service. To you, it means that the party can start and end on time. No child will come in too late for the first games, and linger overlong because Mother hasn't come to pick him up.

Even this solution has its problems. The child may not be ready at the appointed time. His mother may insist that you come in to the house for a short visit. Worst of all, she may not be there when you bring him back! And these problems may arise, whether you come by car, or provide a responsible teen-ager to "walk" the child to and from the party.

Party publicity is highly important, even though it will never solve every single problem. Make sure—make *very* sure—that you notify every parent as to:

- The exact time you will pick the child up or arrange for someone to come for him.
- The exact time the party will be over—and be definite about it.
- The exact time the parent may expect him home.

This information should be given, regardless of the age of the child.

NEVER, NEVER

- Take a child on a party trip without telling the parents ahead of time, giving them all the details, and getting permission.
- Allow a small child to cross a street alone, even if you are watching him.
- Deliver a child to a home in which there is no responsible person present to receive him.
- Permit a small child to leave the party unless accompanied by some responsible person, or in the case of an older child, without telephoning the child's parents first for permission to let him leave, or to tell them that he is on his way.
- Use a teen-ager or other responsible person as escort for the children without making sure he knows and accepts the above warnings.

Pleasing Party Parents

Parents are anxious to fit into your plans, are eager for their youngsters to fit into the party, and want them to enjoy every minute of it. You and they will avoid any misunderstanding if you make a special point to tell all:

- When to come.
- Whether to stay.
- When to come back.

- Whether it's a birthday, and if so, any price limit you want to set, such as "It's Bill's fifth birthday, but please don't spend more than fifty cents on a present. You know how children are at that age."

- What sort of clothes will be most appropriate. No mother wants to dress her daughter up in her best pink ruffles, and have it ruined by catsup and charcoal from a backyard cookout. Neither does a mother want to let her daughter appear in corduroy coveralls when the other little girls are in pink ruffles.

- Costumes, if you're using a special theme, like Indians, gypsies, or pirates. Parents will appreciate being told about any costumes far enough ahead to make, buy, or improvise them.

- Whether the party will be indoors or outdoors. It makes a difference in what a child wears.

- Whether he'll need any special gear (bathing suit or skates, for example) .

- What the parent can do to help. And be specific. "Would you mind coming a bit early and helping the youngsters to get out of their snow suits and boots?" Or "You're so good at making things. Will you help the children decorate their Take-Home Bags?" Or "Could you help me serve the refreshments at four o'clock?" Or "Would you mind being on hand to operate the record player for some songs and a story?"

Parents will appreciate your asking about their children's routines, likes and dislikes. Having such information will help you plan a happy time. Find out:

- Whether the child has any major likes or dislikes in party food.

- Whether the child has any diet problems.

- When he usually has his dinner. If it's very early, then you won't want to overload him with sweets. If not, you might like to add sandwiches, soup, or other such food to the ice cream and cake.

- When he usually has his nap. You'll plan your party time before or after that.

- Whether he is used to going to the bathroom alone, or whether he needs help with buttons and zippers.

3

~~~~~~

Small-Fry Etiquette
or "I Want to Go HOME!"

Parties provide an excellent and painless way to teach—and to learn—the basic courtesy that makes good manners. Pre-party discussions, held informally over the dishpan, or around the kitchen table, can help the child, whether he is the host or whether he will be a guest, to meet situations with a minimum of strain. It is often helpful to "act out" the party. "Let's play like I'm John. I come up the walk and knock at the front door," and you do this. The party boy or girl gets into the spirit, and play-acts his or her role. "I answer the bell and open the door, and say, 'Hello, John, come on in.' " "I brought you a present." "Say, that's keen! Thanks!" If the child is the guest, other previews can be played, including the greeting to John and his mother, and the "Thank you for a very nice time. Goodby."

The party is a fine reason for explaining to the child the need for behavior different from what is required in his own home. Explanations as to why he should not wander over the house, open drawers, delve into the refrigerator, or put his feet on the chairs make sense because there is a reason for learning. Learning how to ask when he wants to go to the bathroom will save him embarrassment. So will knowing how to say "Please, may I have some milk?" instead of an imperious "More!"

The primary object in any rules of etiquette is to smooth the

31

way between people, minimizing misunderstandings and mistakes. The child who is relaxed and secure in a party situation is the child who will enjoy it the most himself and provide the best time for the others.

Who's Coming?

When the party is still only a gleam in the eye, the question "Who's coming?" will arise. And there probably will come the vehement statement "Not *him!* I don't like him!" "Him" may be the son of your best friend, or of your next-door neighbor. How can you and the party child arrive at some mutually agreeable and politic decision?

- Agree upon the number of guests, and work from that point.
- Use some recognized social grouping: the child in his class or school, the Sunday School class, the softball team, the dance class. (These groupings are the easiest way.)
- If the boy objects to inviting a certain girl, an all-boy party may be the solution, or in reverse, an all-girl party.
- Limit the geographical area to the apartment house, the block, or such. This also solves problems of transportation.
- Limit the age range. "James is ten, and everyone else is only seven and eight. Won't he be too big and strong to make the games fair for the others?" Or "Maybe you can ask James to go to the ball game with you and Dad. Wouldn't he like that better than a party?"
- Explain—or try to—the way other people think and act in some situations. "Do you know, if James gave a party and didn't invite *you,* I think I'd feel very bad about it. You see, James's mother and I are old friends, and we want you and James to be friends, too."
- Let the party child realize that he will have to invite or explain to anyone else why he *didn't* invite some boy or girl. If he has a good reason, it will be easy. If not, it will be hard.
- Make sure your own prejudices (we all have them!) aren't

behind your reasons for objecting to some of the child's proposals.

The Problem of Presents

Gifts are sometimes party problems. Here again, pre-planning with the child, and parent publicity are both important. Find out the local customs on presents at parties; then accept or modify these customs as you think best. Certain points to consider may include:

• Children *love* presents. Certain occasions *mean* presents to them, such as birthdays and Christmas.

• Children also like to *give* presents. Picking the gift out, buying it, wrapping it, signing the card, and bringing it to the party is part of the fun.

• These two qualities of taking and giving are closely allied. Both benefit by discussion and practice. The generosity of the giver must be met with the appreciation of the taker. And this has to be taught. A child is usually frank in his personal reaction. "That's silly," or "I don't like checkers," or "I wish it was blue; I don't like pink" are comments that may be true, but which don't appreciate the thought behind the gift, or the feelings of the giver. Learning how to give graciously and to accept graciously are real arts, and they can be learned while young, with adult guidance. Perhaps it will help to try a switch-over. The party child provides a little gift, all prettily wrapped, to exchange with each of his guests.

• If you are in a neighborhood where lots of children mean lots of parties, presents can represent a real expense. Agree with the parents whose children are coming that the gifts should be "token," and not cost more than a half-dollar, or whatever is best. Then stick to it, and mention it often enough to have it kept in mind and observed in practice.

• Where there are no restrictions on gifts, and your budget is limited, let ingenuity replace expense. Look for the unique, unusual, foreign, clever little gifts that will be novel to the child and easy on your purse.

• Set an example by giving no prizes or making them very simple ones—a lollipop, stick of gum, foil-wrapped candy, candy bar, and the like.

4

Party-proofing the House
or "I Didn't Mean to Do It."

"Don't cry over spilt milk" and "Accidents *will* happen" are not much consolation when a young guest gets a big bump on his head from the table corner, or your favorite vase crashes to the floor, or your new slipcovers are spotted with chocolate. It is almost impossible to prevent some spills, spots and smears, but you can minimize them by anticipating the worst ones and taking steps to prevent them.

Don't blame the children. They come with a single thought—to have fun at a party—and they throw themselves into every game without thinking of accidents. They are too young to have developed a sense of value of possessions, or to know that an object can have antique or sentimental value, as well as value in dollars.

Your child is the host or hostess. It is *his* home, too, and you want him to be proud of it. It should look party-like and gay, so when you party-proof it, don't make it look as stark and functional as an operating room! If you stop to think, you will remember that the clean-up after your adult parties always shows a few cigarette burns, white rings on the furniture, and the like. Why expect more of children?

The main object of party-proofing is really *child*-proofing to prevent physical accidents. A few precautions will help:

• Remove any small rugs from bare floors. They'll skid out from under a running child. Also, they're too much fun. The games will turn into sliding contests.

• Disconnect the cords of any lamps not in use, and put them away. Make sure that the cords of lamps in use are out of the way of children's feet. They're easy to stumble over.

• Furniture with sharp corners, such as tables, should be moved in such a way as to get those corners out of the traffic lines of play.

• Loose or hanging tableclothes, scarves, mats and the like are booby traps. A child can clutch at them in running or catching his balance, and have the contents of the table or shelf come down upon his unwary head.

• Place any flower arrangements or other decorations in well-balanced containers out of reach of the children.

• If any theme or game requires a mask, be sure that the eyeholes are wide enough for the child to see through well, and the nose and mouth openings are large enough to allow him to get plenty of air. No thin rubber.

• Supervise the stairs, if there are any. Many of today's children are not used to them. Even when they are, the excitement of the party makes them careless in going up and coming down.

• Never use a game that involves carrying any sharp object in the mouth or hands.

• Be very careful in using any game that requires hurried eating. Small children can choke easily in such situations.

• In a blindfold game, be sure to set limits so that the child who is "it" will not run into a wall, chair or other object. In the case of small children, a paper bag over the head is less frightening than a blindfold, because a bit of the floor will be visible. No plastic over the head!

• Some children are too shy or get too excited by the games to tell you they need to use the bathroom. Be on the look-out for the usual signs, and be ready to take quick action. (One mother makes a practice of keeping a small supply of little cotton panties on hand—just in case!)

• It is not unusual for a child to get so excited that he or she "up-chucks." Be ready to soothe and clean the child, and have supplies handy for a quick mop-up job. Chances are, the child will feel better at once. If not, put him to bed in a quiet room, keeping him warm and quiet.

• Have a first-aid kit handy, complete with cotton and cotton swabs, gauze for bandages, and the brightest band-aids you can find. They're a big help in stopping tears over a scratched knee or finger.

As to protecting the furniture and household articles, the best rule is to "clear the decks for action" without sacrificing the party look.

• Remove any small, valuable or fragile objects from the party area. They can be jarred down, even if no one touches them.

• Remove any articles of furniture that are not needed, or that take up play space. Coffee tables, for example, are more useful to adults than to children.

• If you plan any activity involving the use of scissors, supervise it. The fascination of *cutting* is much greater to a child than *what* he is cutting. He can go from the paper given him to the curtain near him or to the cat's tail!

• If you plan any activity involving the use of crayons, paints, pencils and the like, supervise! There again, for a young child the act of making marks is more important to him than where he makes them. The doors or walls are fine places to paint or write on. You can handle this in several ways: encourage putting the paper and paints on the easy-to-mop floor, cover the wall with big sheets of paper and plan to use it, provide adequate table space and use a plastic cover or layers of newspapers.

• Any sofa or chair with expensive or delicate upholstery or slipcovers can be seen but protected if you cover it with a see-through plastic cloth.

• If any parts of the house are off limits, mark them well, lock the door, or tack a ribbon across them.

And finally, remember that your child, like you, has possessions that he treasures. Those that are too beloved to be shared—and perhaps scratched, torn or broken—should be put away safely out of sight.

5

❧❧

Party Food
or "When Do We EAT?"

Food of some sort is basic to all parties. Offering and sharing food is the universal gesture of friendship.

At a children's party, food is of primary importance. Often it involves not only a meal of some sort, but special food items such as cookies, lollipops and the like that are used as prizes and favors.

Children are not overly critical. They like most what they are most familiar with, so keep the food simple, but provide lots of it. A children's party is not the time to try out new recipes or ingredients unfamiliar to the child. They are food conformists. Of course you can dress the food up and make it look festive.

Although this chapter does not attempt to provide menus and recipes, it includes a few simple ideas that *work*. They are included merely to act as samples. Supplement them from the numerous cookbooks, and the excellent party food ideas in most of the women's magazines. Newspapers and food advertisements are other excellent sources for ideas.

When serving small children, serve small portions and provide "seconds" as needed. Some youngsters dawdle over too much food at one time. See that any meat or vegetable is bite-size. Don't overseason, especially with pepper and other spices.

Whenever possible, serve sit-down food. Children do not have the coordination or the experience to handle plates, glasses, utensils and the like on trays or laps. (Who does?)

Plastic or paper tablecloths can be pretty as well as practical. Plastic or paper dishes are good china-savers, and make cleaning-up time much easier. Bibs for younger children should be supplied. They can be like the ones that restaurants supply for lobster-eaters, or improvised from paper, plastic or cloth. Eating utensils should be suited to the child's size and handling ability. Plastic or paper spoons, knives and forks are not very easily handled. Your silver or stainless steel will be better.

Main Dish Favorites

The all-time favorites of children are hot dogs and hamburgers, whether cooked outdoors on the grill or over the campfire, or on the kitchen stove. Luckily, they are simple, nourishing, and can be partied up.

Hot dogs can be sliced shish-kebab fashion, bite-size, with slices of orange, pineapple, onion, or other tidbits. They can be served on the usual toasted roll, along with a number of different garnishes—catsup, pickle relish, mustard, sauerkraut—whatever are the current favorites. They can be served bite-size, topped with a chunk of cheese, grilled, or as is. They can be grilled with a slice of cheese around them (the old camp pig-in-a-blanket) or slit, stuffed with a slice of cheese and then grilled. Or wrapped in bacon and grilled.

The old standby, the hamburger, is equally popular and versatile. Most children like it fairly well done. Serve it as miniatures—small meatball-style on small rolls or biscuits. Serve it flat, pancake-style on bread or roll, with all sorts of garnishes to choose from.

Chicken can be prepared ahead of time. The drumstick, eaten by hand, is the favorite piece. Creamed chicken on bite-size toasted bread bits is nourishing and good.

Cold cuts of meat come in handy for some parties. They can be spread with cheese, rolled up, and chilled until needed, then cut into bite-size slices. Or combine with peanut butter, cream cheese, jelly, or other favorite spread to make thin, small sandwiches to be served alone or with soup.

Bacon combines beautifully with most meats and cheeses, and can serve as decoration. Half a hot dog bun spread with peanut butter and jelly, topped with a slice of bacon and a paper sail on a toothpick, makes a gay little sandwich "boat."

Casserole-type food is popular, especially if it is spaghetti and meatballs, or macaroni and cheese. A green salad and fruit of some kind, either as a drink or dessert, goes well with these dishes.

Soups are fine where the meal should be light but nourishing. Serve the kind that you know the children like best, very probably cream of tomato, cream of chicken, alphabet noodle, or other hearty sort. If possible, serve in cups, not bowls. They're easier for small hands to handle. Be sure the soup and the cup are not too hot. Tiny tidbits of toast, ham, cheese or bacon will dress it up a bit. Small squares of toast, topped with cheese, cold meat or peanut butter, go nicely with soup. These plus a green salad and dessert make a nourishing meal.

Desserts

Ice cream is a tradition for most children's parties. The two most popular flavors, and the safest in pleasing everybody, are chocolate and vanilla. Try serving ice cream various ways:

• In molds to suit the holiday or occasion. An ice cream bunny, heart, flower, or Santa brings oohs and ahhs.

• The little ice cream cups are always popular, and easy for children to handle.

• A big bowl, full of scoops of different kinds and colors, looks very gala and offers the delicious opportunity of choosing.

• Serve in bowls, and provide several different toppings, such as hot fudge sauce, crushed pineapple, maraschino cherries (red and green), fruit cocktail mixture, well-drained, and any other current or local favorites.

• Add glitter. Prepare a sheet of stiff, brightly colored gelatin (or several sheets of different colors). When firm, chop into tiny bits and sprinkle over the ice cream. It will glow and twinkle and look very glittery.

• Add stick-ins. Any edible or decorative items that can be speared with a toothpick and stuck into the ice cream. Possible items are marshmallows, gumdrops, small flags, sails, tiny toy animals, name tags and the like.

Cake is to ice cream what Jack is to Jill. It is usually considered a must, especially for birthdays. Like ice cream, it can be decorated and served in many different ways.

• Baked in a ring pan, such as used for angel food cakes. Place a glass jar in the center and fill with real or artificial flowers. This makes a pretty cake for an all-girl, or girl's birthday party.
• Decorated with a circus ring of iced animal crackers.
• Decorated with small flags.
• Iced with the child's name and birth date.
• Served individually in the form of cupcakes, decorated with fancy icing.
• Topped with candles. A must for birthday cakes, and make sure the number of candles are those of the child's years. They'll count! If using cupcakes for a birthday party, put a candle on each, but a larger, different-colored one on the birthday child's cupcake. Let the birthday child decide upon the kind of cake he wants.

Cookies

Cookies are musts for children's parties. They are versatile. They can be used as prizes, as placecards, as decorations, as take-homes, even as games (see Chapter 6). They are easy to buy, to make, and to decorate. Try some of the following ideas:

• Initial cookies. Make your favorite cookie dough or use a prepared cookie mix. Prepare enough dough to make a large, fairly thick cookie for each child. Go through the guest list, and cut out a cookie letter, using each child's initial—S for Susie and Sam, D for Dave and Donnie. Decorate each of these initial cookies with colored icing. Or make the usual round cookies but add the child's initials in icing on each one. You can use piecrust instead of cookie dough for initial cookies if you prefer. Children enjoy these personalized cookies. You might put each in a plastic bag so it can be taken home.

• Good luck cookies make nice favors for the older child. Cut the dough into good luck shapes, such as four-leaf clovers and horseshoes.

• Holiday shapes for cookies are always good. Cut the dough into symbolic shapes: eggs and rabbits for Easter and spring; hearts, arrows and cupids for Valentine's Day; shields and stars for patriotic holidays; cats, pumpkins, bats and scarecrows for Halloween; Santa, toys, stockings and stars for Christmas. Use appropriate colors for icing. Or make regular cookies, but add the symbols by using icing.

• Fortune cookies are great fun for the older youngsters. You probably can buy them from a local Chinese or Japanese restaurant, or specialty shop.

Jello

Jello is a light, pretty, easy-to-make and popular dessert for children. They prefer molds, or to have trimmings added, such as crushed fruit or whipped cream.

Pies

Pies are popular, especially with boys, and for non-birthday parties. Popular with children are:

• Apple pie, served hot, with cheese slices or whipped cream.
• Cherry pie, the redder the better.
• Banana cream and chocolate cream pies, topped with whipped cream.

• Best of all, the Jack Horner pie, a covered, pielike affair with ribbons leading to each child's place. A pull—and there's a present or a favor!

Beverages

Party drinks can be coolers or warmers, or both! They are a big part of party food.

• Milk is basic. It can be served plain, with fancy straws to make it gala (see Chapter 6), or it can be chocolate milk. For older children who can be trusted with the electric beater or blender, milk shakes made of various ingredients set out for their use are fun to make.

• Ice cream sodas for the older set are fun to make, too. Set out various syrups, cold soft-drink mixers, ice cream and ice cream scoops, and let them concoct their own. Get Dad to be the soda jerk for the younger set. Ingredients can include chocolate and maple-flavored syrups; frozen fruit slices such as peaches, berries, and the like; various colas, root beer, ginger ale, milk, fruit juices, etc. Add nuts and maraschino cherries for toppings.

• Soft drinks come in all sorts of flavors. Select those most popular with the children. They might include the fruit-flavored drinks, root beer, ginger ale and the cream sodas.

• Fruit drinks are always safe to use, especially those familiar to the children. Orange juice, lemonade (make it pink!) or grape juice are usually popular.

• Hot drinks are fine for winter parties, and for cool, outdoor evenings. Cambric tea, made by mixing hot milk, water and sugar, is the typical little girls' tea-party drink. Grape juice heated with a few cloves makes a spicy hot drink. Vary with other fruit juices, or combine flavors. Hot chocolate and cocoa are both favorites. Top with whipped cream or marshmallow, and add a dash of cinnamon for party flavor.

Girl Scout chocolate coffee makes a pleasant mixture with a grown-up air about it. For four full cups, combine two table-spoons of instant coffee, ¼ cup of sugar, ¼ teaspoon of salt, two squares of unsweetened chocolate, one cup of water and three cups of milk. Stir in a saucepan over low heat until the chocolate is melted. Simmer for four minutes, stirring constantly. When piping hot, remove from stove and beat with a rotary beater until frothy. Pour into cups and top with a glob of whipped cream.

6

Party Perk-ups
or *"Can We Have Balloons?"*

Here are some ideas for easy-to-make or easy-to-do decorations, favors or other party gear. Some can be made ahead of time by the family, the class, or the party boy or girl. Don't worry about not making them perfectly. Children judge by the effect, or the use, not by perfection of detail. Originality also does not impress most children. They enjoy the bold, bright and funny. They also like the unexpected, the surprise, such as the golden walnut that holds a small gift, the initial cookies suggested in Chapter 5, and the make-it-while-you-wait items described in Chapter 7.

Party perk-ups are not difficult to find. Your public library will have many books on children's craft projects made from inexpensive or scrap materials. Women's magazines often carry articles and photographs of table and room decorations and simple gifts, many of which are just what you need. Simplify them if they are too involved or expensive. It is the *effect* that you want to get.

The Front Door

All you have to do is decorate it! It's the first thing a guest will see and can set off the first spark of success. Doors can be decorated in any one of many different ways. A few ideas:

46

• Suspend a bunch of bright balloons by a string that goes over the top of the door and is anchored by a strip of masking tape on the inside (a good way to handle any lightweight decoration—no nails) .

• A big sign in bright colors, saying "PARTY HOUSE."

• A net bag full of foil-covered candies, or lollipops.

• Holiday cut-outs, such as a jack-o'-lantern or witch on broomstick for Halloween, Santa for Christmas, heart for Valentine's Day, star for the Fourth of July.

• Theme cut-outs, such as a Mother Goose character, paper dolls, bunny, or birthday cake.

• Name plates on strings, or leis for each child, looped over the door knob, or on a hook by the door. Each child may take one as he enters.

Party Straws

Materials needed: A supply of colored plastic soda straws and small styrofoam balls, one for each guest. Glue. Odds and ends of decorations.

To make: Poke a hole through the styrofoam ball, using a nail or other object that will make the hole large enough to insert the straw through it. Put a bit of glue on the straw about an inch from the end. Slip the ball over the straw. Let dry.

Then add sequins, bits of ribbon, yarn, paper or other decorations to dress up the ball into the head of an animal, or a clown, boy, girl, or other object. Make them gay and bright. They will make any drink taste better.

Break-opens

Materials needed: An English walnut for each guest. A supply of tiny gifts. Paint or foil paper. Glue.

To make: Open each walnut carefully, take out the nut and connecting tissue, insert the little gift, and glue the halves together. Then paint, gild or wrap the walnut in bright foil. Fill a basket with them, and as each young guest leaves, let him select one to take home. Possible inserts: marbles, bright new dime or penny, charm or ring from the dime store, miniature dolls, cars, or other play equipment. For girls, especially at a slumber party, short fortunes, rolled up and put into the shells, can be substituted.

Cookie Paints

Materials needed: Lots of plain, undecorated cookies, homemade or bought. Paper cups or small jars to contain cookie paints in different colors. Pastry or fairly stiff paint brushes. Protection for the table and floor.

To make: Combine an egg yolk with $\frac{1}{2}$ teaspoon water. Add 3 cups powdered sugar, 3 tablespoons milk, and $\frac{1}{2}$ teaspoon vanilla. Mix thoroughly. Divide this white "paint" into several paper cups or small jars, and add a bit of food coloring to each.

To use: Give each child several cookies and a brush and let him make up the decoration. Or you can specify "anything that reminds you of Christmas," or "Easter," or "Halloween." Of course the cookies go into a boodle bag (see Chapter 7), for takehome favors.

This recipe will make enough cookie paint to decorate all the cookies made from a standard-size box of cookie mix. For a party, you'll have to increase it, depending upon the size of the cookies, the amount of decoration, and the number of children. One cookie can be decorated with about a teaspoon of cookie paint.

Pumpkin Fortunes I

Provide a big real or imitation pumpkin jack-o'-lantern or other container. Place it just inside the front door. Fill it with fortunes made by writing a simple fortune on a small sheet of memo paper, rolling it up and tying it with colored ribbon. These can be made ahead of time by the youngsters giving the party.

To play: Invite each youngster, as he comes inside, to draw his fortune, and either read or have it read to him. Keep them short.

Print or type them if possible, and make them simple, such as: "You will have three children before you are thirty years old," "Fifteen is your lucky number," "Avoid having an argument on July 18," "You will take a long trip soon," "You will get your secret wish," "You will receive a very interesting telephone call soon."

Silhouettes

(This makes a good early-bird activity, too. See Chapter 7.)

Materials needed: As many sheets of white drawing or construction paper as there are guests. Or the regular silhouette paper, black on one side, white on the other. It's nicer, but more expensive. Pencil or chalk. A strong spotlight, lamp or flashlight. Scissors. Glue or paste.

To make: Each child takes his turn sitting very still about six inches from a wall or drawing board on which the paper has been thumbtacked or attached with masking tape (it pulls off neatly). Move the light in such a way as to throw a sharp shadow of the child's profile of head and face onto the paper. Someone with a steady hand outlines this profile on the paper, cuts it out, and then mounts it on a sheet of black paper (or white paper, if the silhouette was drawn on black paper).

Named and dated, it makes a wonderful party take-home. Parents love them, and they can be framed or added to the family scrapbook. "SUSAN ANDERSON, at Donald Jones's party, June 14, 19___." "DONALD, on his sixth birthday, June 14, 19___."

Prizes and Favors

Lots! Lots! LOTS of them! The younger the child, the less he understands losing. The older the child, the more he likes to win a prize. Be on the look-out for suitable small items to use as prizes and favors. Keep them simple and inexpensive. Here are some things children like:

• Miniature items (tiny toy cars, small baskets, little plastic bottles, doll-size parasols, fans, toy furniture, toy kitchen equipment, little brooms and rakes, small boxes of candy and cookies.

• Gadgets (pencils that write with several colors, key rings, small locks with keys, flashlights, little notebooks) .

• Game and play equipment (marbles of different sizes and colors, jacks, jumping ropes, hoops, balls, doll clothes, doll furniture, crayons, stuffed animals, kites, dolls) .

• Puzzles (the ones that have small balls to jiggle into special holes, the interlocking metal ones, wooden ones) .

• Picture books, coloring books, comic books, story and song records.

• Dress-up decorations (paper leis, big-bead necklaces, badges, headdresses of all sorts, masks, big cowboy or Island hats, cowboy neckerchiefs, railroad and baseball caps, plastic bracelets) .

• Candy, especially chocolate bars, anything in bright-colored paper, licorice sticks, peppermint sticks, candy corn, lollipops. Also chewing gum and bubble gum. Unshelled peanuts.

• Cookies, in boxes or separate. Decorated cookies, animal crackers, Crackerjack, popcorn, cupcakes.

• Fruit, especially the sort they're most accustomed to— apples, for example. Bananas are usually great favorites.

Special Entertainment

When the party is a large one, it sometimes helps to enlist the services of people with special talents, or to widen the scope of the party by adding a special treat, trip, or event. These will vary, according to the locality and your budget. Here are popular types:

• Puppeteers, bringing a special puppet show at a given time.

• A storyteller, dressed as Mother Goose, the Pied Piper, a gypsy or other character, who arrives at a given time, preferably just before or after the meal. He or she tells stories for from fifteen minutes to an hour, depending on the ages of the youngsters.

• A magician, to put on a magic show.

• A play leader, to conduct the party games (a playground leader in the local recreation agency might be a good choice) .

• Pony rides. These can *make* a party for young children if you have the space, and can find someone who has a pony, and who will take charge.

• Home movies. The home movie of the last birthday or other party will enthrall the youngsters. Or rent some films suitable for the group. Animal stories and cartoons are always popular.

Trips and Other Out-of-the-House Activities

These require the consent of the parents and good supervision. Provide an adult or responsible older teen-ager for every six or eight youngsters in the older age group, and for every four to six in the younger. The younger the children, the shorter the trip.

It is a good idea to take a roll of paper towels or a box of paper handkerchiefs. You'll need them for wiping fingers and faces, and for possible car sickness. Also find out the location of service station rest rooms and building or agency bathrooms ahead of time. Someone *always* has to go. Possible places to visit are:

• The public library, for storytelling.
• The nearest amusement park.
• A children's zoo.
• The local club or neighborhood swimming pool.
• The local movie.
• The park. Some parks have special party areas designed especially for children, and which provide the leadership, refreshments and favors for children's parties at very moderate cost per child. Check to see if there are any in your vicinity.
• The beach. Here again, provide lots of supervision.
• The children's theatre or puppet theatre for some special play or show.

Such special trips can be the main attraction for the party, or just part of it. In any case, decorations, favors and food will play a big role in its success.

PART II

P(ARTY) DAY

or

"It's Too Late to Back Out Now!"

The three chapters in this section suggest party ACTION. Action means ACTIVITIES—from the moment the child arrives to the last goodby from the last child to leave for home.

Waiting-around activities to keep early-comers in the party spirit are sometimes hard to find or to devise. Many here involve amusing make-it-yourself activities.

Active party games, some suitable for the younger, some for the older youngsters, have been chosen either for their traditional appeal or for their novelty. They are all simple to conduct, require very little in equipment, and in many cases may be played either indoors or outdoors. Needless to say, they may also be used at picnics, in camp, in the schoolroom, gym, or playground. Best of all, however, they are party FUN.

The chapter on less active games will fill the need for quiet-down play useful before or after eating, and as a change of pace when youngsters begin to be overexcited or tired.

As a general guide to the age levels of the games, four broad groupings have been used, and will be shown after each game title. They include:

ALL—any age (with possible slight modifications)
VY—very young (approximately 4-6)
SO—slightly older (approximately 7-9)
AT—almost teens (approximately 10-12)

Of course, children just *won't* stay in any one classification, so use your own judgment, and select, adapt or modify games to suit your own party group.

7

❧❧

SOMEBODY Has to Be First
or *"Isn't Anybody ELSE Coming?"*

The first half-hour of a party can be decisive. Every party has its early-birds—youngsters who for one reason or another arrive before the others. If they wander around, waiting for the others to arrive, the party spirit will fall flat. Make them welcome. Have plans for keeping them happy and busy from the minute they come through the front door.

Early-bird activities should be a real part of the party, getting everybody involved, and making the early arrivals feel important. They can give the youngsters the fun of making things for themselves or for the party.

When, however, everyone has arrived, and even the last to come have had a taste of these activities, leave them and get on with the action.

Balloon Birds   ALL

Materials needed: At least one long balloon per child, allowing extras for breakage. Pieces of colored paper cut into strips for feathers, legs, wings, tails and eyes. Glue. Blunt scissors.

To make: Leave the end of the balloon unblown. This makes the beak. The youngsters select and glue the paper slips to the "bird" to make its wings, legs, eyes, tails.

55

Substitute: Instead of birds, the youngsters can make animals, clowns, pirates or other characters out of round balloons.

Boodle Bags   ALL

Materials needed: A small paper bag for each child. Crayons. Pages of bright, slick paper ads. Blunt-tipped scissors. Paste.

To make: Place supplies on a table. As each child arrives, give him a paper bag, and let him decorate it any way he likes, with crayons and cut-outs. If the child is old enough to read and recognize letters, encourage him to find the letters that spell his name, and to paste them on his bag, so that he can take his own bag home when the party is over.

Substitute: Small shopping bags make nice boodle bags. Advertisements on them can be covered with paper cut-outs.

For holidays, encourage appropriate cut-outs. Little girls—and boys, too—like to add glitter by gluing sequins and using spray cans. Supervise!

Children's Zoo   VY

Materials needed: Large paper bags, the big ones that will go over a child's shoulders, one for each child. No plastic! Crayons. Scissors. Wool, felt, fur, paper, and any other odds and ends for decoration.

To make: As each child arrives, "measure" him for an animal. Put the bag over the child's head and shoulders, mark the location of the child's face inside, remove the bag, and cut out a square or circle large enough to let the child's entire face show. Then you and the child decorate the bag to make some wild, weird and wonderful animal, using any of the odds and ends. Cut the length of the bag to allow easy, safe walking.

To play: When everyone has made and "become" an animal, hold a zoo parade around the play area or the block. Or play "circus." Each animal puts on a demonstration of the way he acts. Youngsters take the costumes home as part of the favors.

Substitutes: Lightweight cardboard boxes. Garment bags, *if not plastic.*

For a party for little girls, cut openings in suit or dress dry cleaning bags for head at the top and arms at shoulder height. Then cut the bottom off at ankle length. They decorate their "dress" in any style they like: evening dress, "mod," animal, clown, fairy-tale character, for example. Then encourage dramatic play in the paper outfits. Take a walk around the block in them. Hold a ball, or a dance.

Citrus Sillies   SO, AT

Materials needed: An orange, lemon or grapefruit for each child. Colored scraps of paper to cut into eyes, ears, noses, whiskers, teeth, tails and other animal features. Glue or tape to attach them to the fruit. Cardboard. Pipe cleaners and other odds and ends.

To make: Put all the supplies on a table. As each child arrives, give him a grapefruit, and tell him he can make any animal he likes. Give him ideas for using the paper scraps, but let him design his own animal. Set each in a cardboard collar, made of a length of cardboard folded and stapled to make a ring in which the fruit will sit without rolling. Place the finished animals on exhibition. Everybody takes his animal home when the party is over.

Egg Animals   ALL

Materials needed: A big bowlful of hardboiled eggs, or styrofoam eggs. Pipe cleaners. Bits of string, ribbon, felt and other odds and ends. Glue. Crayons.

To make: Each youngster makes and decorates his own egg animal, bug, fish, butterfly or other creature, using his choices of the scraps. Exhibit them on table or mantle. Use them as take-homes when the party is over. You can also allow the children free choice, or limit the egg forms to seasonal, holiday or special party theme.

Frog Goggles   VY

Materials needed: Egg cartons, the kind with molded depressions for the eggs. A goggle requires two such depressions. A carton holding a dozen eggs will provide the makings of six frog goggles.

To make: Cut out the carton area into six two-hole sections. Attach an elastic band or string at the corners of each goggle, to hold the goggle in place over the eyes. Cut a hole in the center of each depression, big enough for the child to see well. Decorate the "frog eyes." Then play hopping games of the relay and tag type. These "frog eyes" can also be decorated to make very weird "moon men" for a space theme.

Flying Saucers   SO, AT

Materials needed: A wire coathanger. Crepe paper, ribbon, tinsel or other decoration. String and nail for hanging. Small paper plates for the flying saucers.

To make: Pull the long straight bottom edge of the hanger down until the hanger becomes a round loop, with the hook at the top. Decorate it if you like with tinsel for Christmas, red paper heart hung from it for Valentine's Day, black cat cut-out for Halloween, for example. Hang the loop from the center of an open doorway by string and nail or tape.

To play: As a youngster arrives, give him five small paper plates. He stands about ten feet away and tries to sail his saucer through the hoop. Five points for each successful try—or a small prize, such as a lollipop or balloon for each successful throw.

Variations: Hang a bell from the center of the hoop. Players try to hit it and make it ring. Or tape several of the hoops together and give each a different score—five points for the center hoop, three for the top, two for the bottom, for example.

Use ping-pong balls, soft rubber balls, beanbags or other substitutes for the paper plates. The younger the child, the shorter should be the throwing distance, the larger the hoop and the easier the object to toss.

For outdoors, use a barrel hoop hung from a tree, and increase the throwing distance. Appoint some youngsters to act as ball retrievers.

Ghost Trail   vy, so

Provide a magic string for each guest. One end is free. The other is tied to some object and has a small prize or favor there. Set these up ahead of time, crossing the strings, going around furniture, zigzagging, up and over, with the hidden gift end out of sight.

To play: As each child enters, give him the end of one of the strings, and tell him to follow it, going over or under another string when necessary, until he finds the end—and a surprise present.

Live Paper Dolls   vy

Materials needed: A sheet of wrapping paper (any color). Crayons. Blunt-tip scissors. Cord or string.

To make: As each child arrives, he or she is "measured" for a paper doll. The child lies down on the paper. You or one of the youngsters (perhaps the host) outline the child's body with crayon. Then each child (if old enough) cuts out his own outline, and "dresses" it by using the crayons to indicate hair, face, and clothes. The finished paper doll is then attached to the string with masking tape or by stapling, and the string is hung along a wall or other area. When the party is over, each child takes his paper doll home.

Name Lines   vy, at

Materials needed: A large index card, or a piece of cardboard, or heavy paper, about 4" x 6" in size, for each child. Crayons. Length of cord.

To make: As each youngster arrives, he prints his name on one of the cards, then decorates it as he pleases. It is then hung or stapled to the length of cord that is strung across the room, or along a wall. When the party is over, each child takes his name card home.

Variations: Each child draws his pet, or a pet he'd like to have. Or draws a clown's face, a bunny, a reindeer, or other seasonal or holiday symbols.

Play Jewelry   SO, AT

Materials needed: Pages of gay, slick-paper ads from magazines. Scissors, blunt-tipped for under-eights. Paste. Rulers. String for earring loops. Bottle caps. Odd buttons. Macaroni in various shapes. Tinfoil. Soft wire. Beads from broken necklaces. Any other pretty odds and ends.

To make: For little girls, show them how to cut the paper into small triangles of various sizes and shapes. Then spread the wrong side of the triangle lightly with paste and roll it from the wide or base end toward the narrow end. This makes the bead thickest in the center. Let the beads dry; then string them into necklaces. Hang on short loops over the ears for earrings. Combine with other beads, buttons, macaroni, and other odds and ends, if you like. (Older girls might like to apply a coat of clear shellac to the beads after they are thoroughly dry. It gives the necklace a fine shine.) Use wider, larger paper triangles for making bead belts.

For boys, decorate a bottle top with foil, or a gold star. Remove the cork, push the boy's shirt into the cap, and push the cork into it from the inside of the shirt. Presto! A sheriff! Curtain rings on string loops make good pirate or gypsy earrings. The paper beads described above make good belts for pioneer or Indian tunics. Also for decorations for ankles, amulets, and the like.

Twirlers   VY, SO

Materials needed: Eight-inch squares of bright, shiny paper. Straight pins. Corks from the caps of soft drink bottles. Sticks, about a foot long (dowels, garden stakes, tree branches). Blunt-tipped scissors. Pencils and rulers for drawing cutting lines.

To make: As each child arrives, give him a paper square, and show him how to draw a line from corner to corner, diagonally. Then show him how to cut along these lines, up to about 2″ of the center. He then brings alternate corners up to the center, sticks the pin through the cork, and then into the end of the stick. The paper should move easily on the pin.

To play: Youngsters like to run with these "windmills" and watch them twirl in the wind. Let each child demonstrate his twirler. Children can "play act" being airplanes, with full sound effects. Take-home favor.

Substitute: Full-page, colored ads from slick-paper magazines make gay twirlers. For young children, work with each, to avoid overcutting, and finger-sticking.

Blind Choice   ALL

A nice way to give a party favor to a new arrival or to the guests just before they leave. Provide a pretty gift, all party-wrapped, for each guest. Hang them all by strings or ribbons from a clothesline or cord stretched between doors, trees, or other objects.

To play: As each child arrives, tell him he can have whatever package he chooses from the line. Blindfold him with cloth or paper bag, turn him toward the line, and tell him to go forward and choose his package. He goes forward, fumbles until he finds a package, then holds onto it while you take off his blindfold and cut the package from the line. If the party is for girls and boys, make sure the gifts are suitable for both, or provide two lines, one for girls, the other for boys.

Butterfingers   SO, AT

Materials needed: Pennies (bright, new ones are more fun).

To play: As each child arrives, ask him to hold out one hand, palm up. Place a penny on each fingertip (not the thumb). Each child must try to get all the pennies into one pile on one fingertip, *not using thumb or other hand*. Any pennies dropped must be picked up and replaced where they were. Anyone who succeeds gets to keep the pennies.

What makes it click: Novelty. Self-challenge. Concentration.

Squeeze It   SO, AT

Materials needed: Three or more oranges and a wastebasket or box.

To play: As each child arrives (this stunt is better for boys than for girls), place three oranges in front of him on the floor. Tell him he will be timed. At a signal, he must bend down, pick up one orange with his knees, hobble over to the basket or box and drop the orange in it without using his hands. He must then come back, pick up the second orange, take it to the box, etc. Keep a careful time record for each boy, and when each has had his turn, announce the winner. In case of a tie, the two top winners compete for first place.

Variation: This is a good stunt to use with a few contestants, the other guests as spectators.

What makes it click: Humor. Novelty. Physical agility.

What Am I?   VY

Materials needed: As many animal crackers as there are guests. Try to get a wide variety of animals. Wrap each in a piece of bright tissue, twisting the ends. Place them all in a big bowl or basket.

To play: As each child arrives, ask him to take one of the pieces from the bowl, but not to open it until everyone has arrived. Then get them all into a circle. Each then unwraps his animal without letting anybody see what it is. In turn, each child then goes inside the circle and acts like his animal. The others try to guess what animal it is. Encourage the acting and the guessing, so as to break the party ice.

ID Cards   ALL

Materials needed: A file card for each child. Ink pad. Bathroom scales. Yardstick. Cellophane or saran wrap.

To make: As each child arrives, he must get his ID card. He steps up to the table where you are sitting. You ask him, *very* seriously, his name, address and age, writing it all down on his card. Then, with ceremony, you weigh him, measure his height, and put all that on his card. On the back of the card, he puts his fingerprints, using the ink pad to get his fingers all nicely inked, then rolling them across the card in the most approved police manner. Then cover his ID card with the cellophane or saran, and it is his for keeps.

Cup Dolls   VY, SO

Materials needed: A number of paper cups, all sizes and shapes. Odds and ends of yarn, buttons, beads, pipe cleaners, tissue paper, ribbon, etc.

To make: As each little girl arrives, she gets busy making a cup doll, using whatever cups and scraps she likes. Collect them, put them all out on a table or shelf, and have a paper cup doll show. Everyone votes on the prettiest, oddest, funniest, cutest, craziest, etc.

Dash and Dot   SO, AT

Materials needed: A sheet of paper or an index card, and a pencil for each guest.

To play: As each child arrives, give him or her the paper and pencil, and tell him to draw anything he likes, but he must use only twelve lines and one dot. When he has finished, he must sign or initial it, and give it to you. When everyone has arrived and has made his drawing, put them all on view on a table, mantle, or the floor, and let the youngsters vote for the prettiest, the funniest, the scariest, the most unusual, etc. Then everyone takes his drawing home in his boodle bag.

Jet Rocket   VY, SO

Provide a balloon, preferably the sausage-shaped type, for each guest. Draw a circle or a line on the floor or ground. Provide a string or cord for measuring.

To play: As each child arrives, give him a balloon and ask him to blow it up. When this has been done, the child holds it tightly by the neck to keep the air in. He then steps into the circle or up to the line, and lets the balloon jet forward by releasing his fingers. Measure the distance with great care, and make a note of it. When everyone has had his turn, announce the name of the child whose jet went the farthest. A toy airplane or another balloon makes a good prize.

Masks   VY, SO

Materials needed: One paper or aluminum pie plate per child. A supply of clothespins, buttons, pipe cleaners, yarn, paper, and any other odds and ends. Glue, stapler, crayons, etc.

To make: As each youngster arrives, he is invited to sit down, use the materials in front of him, and make a mask, using his own ideas. As each is finished, collect it, and then have a showing. Each child gets his mask to take home with him.

Park It   VY, SO

Supply five or more marbles per guest. Ahead of time, find a good, sturdy cardboard or corrugated board box or carton. Cut five doorways of different width in one of the long sides of the box, and label each with a different point value, the smaller the opening, the higher the value. For small children who can't add large numbers, make the box openings the same size, and just count the number of marbles that go in.

To play: As each child arrives, give him five marbles, and tell him to see how many marbles he can "park" in the box garage. If necessary, help him to add his score, and write it down. When everybody has had a turn, announce the winner, or have play-offs by those with the three highest scores.

Scarecrows   ALL

Materials needed: Large brown paper bags, the kind used at large supermarkets. Lots of old newspapers. Cord or twine. Poster paint.

To make: As the children arrive, set them to work making a scarecrow. The head, a bag stuffed with newspapers. Arms and legs, rolls of newspapers, tied together. Another bag for the body. Legs fastened inside the body bag, tied at the neck. Wool or excelsior for hair. Use paper snips or paint to make eyes, nose, mouth. Any other decorations that will make the scarecrow more impressive. Children can work alone, or in groups. Then, hold a scarecrow show, with all the scarecrows lined up along the sidewalk or front walk. If everybody made one, he may take it home with him. If only one or two were made, keep them as party decorations, or use them for prizes in some of the party games.

8

It's GO All the Way
or "I Speak to Be It!"

Here are the go-go games, the games that "turn on" the party. Here are little dramatic games for the smallies; relays, tags and circle games for the school-agers. Here are games for girls, for boys, and for mixed groups. Some you may know. Some the youngsters will know and expect, because they're considered part of any party.

Play them with enthusiasm. Change them before they get monotonous. See that every child gets a turn at being "it," to be part of a team, and has a fair chance to win. Dramatize them by actions, voice and facial expressions. Play them with humor and zest. They're catching!

Ball Puss-in-the-Corner   so

Materials needed: A large soft ball, beanbag, or small pillow, depending on whether the players are indoors or outdoors. Appoint one player to be Puss.

To play: Each player finds a corner—a tree, post, corner of house, door, furniture or other object. Players change corners at will, and Puss tries to get a corner by hitting a player below the waist with the soft object.

Or Puss can call out "Puss wants a corner!" When he does that, everybody *must* change corners, and Puss tries to tag somebody with the ball. If he succeeds, he takes a corner, and the player who was hit becomes the new Puss.

What makes it click: Excitement, daring, suspense.

Mechanical Dolls   SO, AT

See that each little girl has a boy partner. Mark a starting and a finish line.

To play: The children line up on the starting line, the girls standing rigidly like mechanical dolls. At the signal, the race starts, but the little girls can move their legs *only* when their partners lift each of their feet, place it forward, then the next foot, etc. First "doll" to get to the finish line and back is the winner.

What makes it click: Humor. Boy-girl appeal.

Cavemen   SO, AT

Get the children seated in a big circle, girls on the right of the boys, and one extra chair next to one of the boys. Provide a record with a strong beat, and someone to handle the record player.

To play: When the music starts, the boy next to the empty chair must dash over to any girl of his choice, grab her by her wrists, and pull her over to the empty chair. Just as soon as, but not before, this couple is seated, the boy left with an empty chair by him must dash and bring back *his* girl, and so on. Every now and then, the music stops, and whatever couple is out of their seats at that moment must drop out of the game. Remove their two seats, and resume. Very exciting.

What makes it click: Boy-girl appeal. Suspense.

Chariot Race   SO

Materials needed: Colored streamers of cloth, ribbon or crepe paper. Select a tree, post or other object as a goal or turning point.

To play: Divide the children into groups of three. One of each group is the King or Charioteer; the other two are the King's horses. The horses join inside hands, and hold a streamer end in the outside hand. The King holds the ends of the streamers, making reins. At the signal, each chariot team races to the turning point, goes around it, and races back to the starting line. First to return wins. Try best two out of three. Play very dramatically, with horses pawing the ground at the start, neighing as they go, and the King shouting at them.

Variation: Chariots race *around* the area, and you time them with a stop watch. Run in heats, with winners competing in the final race.

What makes it click: Drama. Color. Peer competition.

Ditch Him!   SO, AT

This is a good game for boys. Get the players into two parallel lines facing each other about two feet apart.

To play: Each boy leans forward, takes the hands of the boy facing him, and they try to pull each other across the ditch. Teammates may help each other. Play about three minutes; then count the players on each team. The side with the most players on its own side of the ditch wins. Play best two out of three.

What makes it click: Aggression. Peer competition.

Bear Walk Relay   SO, AT

Divide the group into relay teams, about four or five players per team, lined up behind a starting line, and facing a finish line about twenty feet away. Indoors, use the far wall as the finish line.

To play: Player #1 on each team bends his knees a bit, bends from his waist and touches the floor with his hands. He must walk like a bear, moving his right hand and left foot, then left hand and right foot, all the way to the finish line, and touch it with his hands. Then he stands up and runs back to touch player #2, who at once starts *his* bear walk. First team to finish the bear walk and get back into place is winner. Play best two out of three.

What makes it click: Competition. Team cooperation. Action. Pantomime.

Blue and White   ALL

Materials needed: A piece of cardboard about the size of the ones used by the laundry in folding shirts. Cover or paint one side of it bright blue, the other side white.

To play: Divide the youngsters into two groups, the Blues and the Whites. Tie a white band on the arm of each White (bandage gauze is fine) . Then stand along a side of the room or playing area, while the youngsters move around, the teams all mixed up. They must watch you as they move around.

Every now and then you hold the cardboard up high, so that everyone can see it. If the blue side shows, all the Blues must squat down quickly, and the Whites try to tag them before they can do so. If the white side shows, all the Whites try to squat before they are tagged by Blues. Those tagged join you on the sideline, or you can count the tags, but keep everyone in the game. Play about five or six times unless the game gets so exciting that it demands more time.

What makes it click: Suspense. Quick reactions. Agility.

Catch of Fish   VY, SO

Draw two safety lines about thirty feet apart. This game works best out-of-doors with lots of running space. If played in a limited space, it works best with only about five players on each side.

To play: Half the players are Fish. The others become a Net by holding hands. At a signal, the Fish and the Net advance toward the center of the playing area. The Net tries to catch as many of the Fish as possible by enclosing them. The Fish try to escape the Net by running around its ends. Fish caught by the Net may not break through anywhere except where its two ends come together. If the Net breaks apart anywhere, all the Fish are safe. All the caught Fish are counted. Play twice; then let the Fish become the Net.

What makes it click: Suspense. Cooperative action. Skillful dodging.

Cat and Mice   VY

Provide a stool or low kitchen stepladder for the Cat to sit on. Appoint one player to be the Cat. The others are Mice.

To play: The Cat sits on the stool, chair or low stepladder with his back to the children. The children sit on chairs or stand back of a safety line, facing the back of the Cat. You silently point to one, two, three or four of the Mice, depending on the number of players. They tiptoe up to the Cat and scratch on his stool or chair. The Cat then dashes to try to catch one of the Mice as they all scramble back to their chairs or safety line. The first Mouse caught becomes the new Cat. Encourage squeaking and meowing.

What makes it click: Suspense. Drama. Fun of outwitting the Cat.

Catch the Cane   SO, AT

Provide a cane, broomstick, yardstick or other straight object about a yard long. Get the players into a circle, or half-circle, if space is limited. Number the players (you *can* use their names, but this game moves faster if numbers are used instead of names).

To play: One person is "it," and stands in the middle of the circle. He rests the cane on the floor, holding it straight with his forefinger. He then calls out any number, and lifts his finger off the cane. The child with that number must run up and try to catch the cane before it falls to the floor or ground. If he succeeds, he becomes "it." If not, the former "it" tries again.

What makes it click: Suspense. Need for close attention. Agility.

Circle Racing   SO

Mark off a good, big circle on floor or ground. This game needs lots of space. Best outdoors.

To play: Youngsters stand on the circle, all facing the same direction, allowing some distance between each player. At a signal, they all start running clockwise, each trying to pass the player just in front of him. If he succeeds, he tags that player as he passes, and the tagged player drops out. The last player untagged is the winner.

What makes it click: Peer competition. Physical action.

Fox and Squirrel   SO

This game is a bit like Dog and Rabbit, but more difficult. They make a good team, starting with the simpler.

Provide two beanbags, or volleyballs. Get the youngsters into two even lines, facing each other about six feet apart (farther for older, more skillful youngsters).

To play: One ball is the Fox, the other the Squirrel. At the signal, the Squirrel is tossed from one end player of one line to the player opposite him. This player tosses it to # 2 in the opposite line, and so on, the Squirrel zigzagging back and forth between the lines. When it gets to the end of the line it is started back up. Right after the Squirrel is started, the Fox is started down the lines in the same manner. Can the Fox catch up with and pass the Squirrel? If either is dropped, the person who touched it last must pick it up and put it back in play.

What makes it click: Suspense. Self-competition. Drama.

Frog in the Sea   VY

Get the youngsters into a large circle. Appoint one or more Frogs. A Frog for every five players makes a fast game.

To play: The Frogs sit inside the circle, their legs folded tailor-fashion. The others dance back and forth, teasing and taunting the Frogs, saying, "Frog in the sea, Can't catch me!" The Frogs try to tag anyone coming too close. When that happens, the tagged player becomes a Frog. Play until the circle gets too small.

What makes it click: **Drama. Teasing. Suspense. Agility.**

Needle and Thread   SO, AT

Get the youngsters into two lines of equal number, facing each other about ten to fifteen feet apart.

To play: Players join hands and number off consecutively. You stand where all can hear you and call off any two consecutive numbers that have been used by the teams. For example, you call "three and four." In each line, players 3 and 4 raise their joined hands to make an arch. Then the players at the head and at the foot of the line run through the arch, the others following with hands still joined. Of course the players making the arch must turn under their own arms, so as not to drop hands. The first team to "thread the needle," that is, go through the arch and straighten out the line, is the winner.

What makes it click: **Quick reactions. Humor. Team spirit.**

Stone   VY, SO

Make a large circle on the floor or ground. Select a safety zone at each end of the playing area.

To play: One player is the Stone. He sits calmly in the center of the circle, biding his time. The others dash in and out, teasing him. Suddenly and unexpectedly Stone jumps up and chases the others who are not safe until they can reach a safety zone. Any player caught becomes another Stone, and goes to the middle of the circle. Play until most of the children are caught. This game is a bit like Frog in the Sea, but is more active. Play them in succession.

What makes it click: **Suspense. Element of chance. Peer competition. Aggression.**

Shoe Shuffle   SO, AT

Materials needed: Two shoe boxes or their equivalent for each team.

To play: Get the youngsters into teams of equal number, lined up behind a starting line. Mark off a finish line about twenty feet away (or almost the length of the room). The first player of each team puts his feet into the shoe boxes, and at the signal, runs (shuffles) to the finish line and back. He then steps out of the boxes, and player # 2 steps into them. So on, until each player has made his run and is back in his original place. The first team to get all of its players in line again is the winner.

What makes it click: Humor. Team spirit. Novelty.

Crocodile Race   SO, AT

Get the youngsters into teams lined up behind a captain. Mark a starting and a finish line, not too far apart, because this is a strenuous race.

To play: The players of each team squat in deep kneebend position, and each puts his hands on the shoulders of the boy in front of him. Each team then hops to the finish line and back. If it falls over (and it probably will), it must return, re-form and start over.

What makes it click: Humor. Agility. Team competition.

Come with Me   VY, SO

Get the youngsters into a fairly close circle. It helps sometimes to draw one on the ground, or mark one on the floor.

To play: One child is "it." He goes around the circle, stops in front of anyone he pleases, and says "Come with me." That child leaves the circle and puts his hands on "it"'s shoulders. Together they move along, stopping in front of other children, and saying "come with me." Finally, when "it" has four or five players behind him, he yells "Go home!" Then everybody rushes to get into one of the empty places in the circle. The one who fails to find an empty place is the new "it."

What makes it click: The tense waiting to be chosen. Suspense. Action. Need to pay close attention.

Copenhagen   VY, SO

Provide a length of rope, cord or ribbon long enough to go all around the circle of children, each holding to it.

To play: Each youngster holds onto the rope or ribbon with both hands, fairly loosely. One player, the Dane, stands inside the circle. The Dane tries to slap the hands of any player holding the rope; the younger the children, the lighter the slap should be. That player tries to drop the rope before his hands are slapped. If his hands get slapped, he becomes the new Dane.

What makes it click: Suspense. Trying to outwit the other. Slight element of aggression.

Cow's Eye   VY, SO

This is an old Chinese game. Get the youngsters into a circle, sitting on the floor with their feet toward the center. Appoint one player to be "it," or be "it" yourself.

To play: Teach the group this Chinese count-out jingle:

> One, two, three, and an old cow's eye,
> When a cow is blind, she'll surely die,
> A piece of shin and a melon too,
> If you have money I'll sell to you;
> But if you're without
> I'll put you OUT!

As "it" chants the rhyme, he goes around the inside of the circle, touching the feet of each child in turn. The foot being touched at the word "out" must be drawn up, and not counted again. If both feet of a child get touched, both must be drawn up. The game goes on until every foot has been touched out.

The child to remain the longest in the game wins, and is "it" for the next go-round.

Variation: When played with the older boys, the last remaining foot in the game gets slapped by all the other players.

What makes it click: Suspense. The appeal of counting-out rhythm. Child humor.

Crackerhead   SO, AT

A good game for boys. Tie a cracker on the head of each boy. Gauze from a bandage roll makes a useful tie. Line them up facing each other behind lines about eighteen inches apart. Provide each player with a rolled-up newspaper sheet.

To play: At the signal, each boy tries to break the crackers on the other boys' heads, while preserving his own. Last boy to have an unbroken cracker wins. Play two out of three.

What makes it click: Peer competition. Humor. Agility.

Musical Madness   VY, AT

Provide a record with a good dance beat, and someone to play it.

To play: Everybody starts walking around the area, keeping time to the music as soon as it starts. When it stops suddenly, everybody must grab a partner, and walk around in twos as the music starts again. At the next sudden stop, partners must change, and everybody must get into groups of threes. Then fours. When the music stops when they are in groups of fours, they go back to walking singly, if the youngsters are very young. For older youngsters, the almost-teens, they may break into twos and dance together.

What makes it click: Boy-girl appeal. Rhythm. Mixer for the shy.

Egyptian Salute   SO, AT

Get the youngsters into two teams, in single file, facing each other. The person at the left end of each line starts the game as soon as he hears the signal. He must touch the top of his head, his nose and one of his feet, using his right hand. He then must make a complete turn, and touch the top of the head of the player on his right. So on, down the line. First team to finish wins the game, but it usually ends in a complete chaos of giggles.

What makes it click: Humor. Concentration. Team spirit.

Dog and Bone   VY

Provide a rubber bone or other small object that won't rattle when picked up. Get the players into a circle. Select a Dog.

To play: The Dog crouches on the floor and hides his head in his arms. Place the bone behind him, and point silently to one of the children to get the bone. That child c-r-e-e-p-s up as noiselessly as possible, takes the bone and rejoins the circle, holding the bone out of sight behind him. All the other players try to look innocent also, and hold their hands behind their backs.

When you tell the Dog that someone has the bone, he turns around, and takes three guesses to name who that person is. If he guesses right, that person is the next Dog. If wrong, he stays Dog for the next round. Small children love to be or stay Dog, so it's a good idea to change Dogs after every two rounds. Encourage growling and barking.

What makes it click: The importance of being the Dog. Suspense in trying to get the bone. Suspense in guessing. Anticipation of being chosen.

Duck, Duck, Goose   VY

Get the children into a circle, all stooping. Appoint "it."

To play: "It" goes around outside the circle, tapping players on the head and saying "Duck" as he does so. When he gets to the player he wants to tag, he touches that player on the head and says "Goose." That player gets up, and chases "it" around the circle, trying to get back into the vacant place. If "it" gets there first, Goose becomes the new "it."

What makes it click: Suspense. Peer competition. Humor. Physical skills.

This Is My Nose   VY, SO

An old game, but it never fails to amuse children. Get the children into a line or circle, and appoint "it."

To play: "It" faces anybody he pleases, points to some part of his own body and calls it by the name of some other part. For example, "it" might say, "This is my head," while pointing to his foot. The person must instantly reply by pointing to his head and saying "This is my foot." If he answers incorrectly, or does not answer before "it" can count ten, he becomes the new "it."

What makes it click: Child humor. Quick reactions. Suspense.

Red-hot Firecracker   SO, AT

Provide a knotted handkerchief or other soft object.

To play: Children sit in a circle, close together. "It" stands in the middle. The children in the circle pass or throw the handkerchief rapidly back and forth around and through the circle, while "it" tries to catch it. When he does, the last player who touched it becomes the new "it." This may be played with beanbag or volleyball, but it goes faster when the "firecracker" is light and not likely to roll.

What makes it click: Element of aggression. Teasing. Agility. Concentration.

Elephant   SO, AT

Get the youngsters into a circle and appoint an "it."

To play: "It" stands in the center of the circle, twirls around, points to some player and calls out "Elephant!" He then starts to count to ten.

The player pointed to must make a trunk by holding his two fists in front of his nose. At the same time the two players next to

Elephant must raise their inside hands to make the Elephant's ears.

Any one of these three players who makes a mistake, or who doesn't make the motions before "it" counts ten, must be the new "it." If they all obey correctly, "it" twirls around, and points to a new Elephant.

What makes it click: Quick reactions. Suspense. Surprise. Humor.

Farmer and the Crow   so

Materials needed: A half-dozen or so small objects (paper plates, beanbags, pieces of cardboard, small boxes or the like) .

To play: Divide the youngsters into two teams, each behind a starting line, facing a wall or finish line about twenty feet away. The first player on each team is a Farmer, the second player a Crow, the third a Farmer, fourth a Crow, and so on.

At a signal, the first Farmer on each team takes the seeds (six beanbags or other small objects) and places them at equal intervals from the starting line to the finish line. He runs back and touches the second player, a Crow. Crow must hop over each of the objects, touch the finish line, change to the other foot, hop back, and pick up each seed as he comes to it. He hands them to player # 3, a Farmer, who goes out to plant them again, and so on. The team finishing first wins. Play again, letting each Crow become a Farmer.

What makes it click: Peer competition. Team Cooperation. Agility.

Follow the Leader   vy

Either be the leader or appoint somebody who is active and resourceful.

To play: Everybody gets in line behind the leader and imitates everything he does. He keeps the line moving, and sets all sorts of actions for them—hopping on one foot, climbing over or under some obstacle, jumping, walking backwards, turning around while walking, skipping, moving his arms, and the like.

What makes it click: Humor. Quick reaction to changing movements. Imitative movement. *Comment:* This is a good way to get the party started, or to get the children to the dinner table, or to get them started homeward, leading them to their wraps, or to the car, and the like.

Frog Race   VY, SO

Mark a goal line from twenty to forty feet away, depending on what space you have. Line the children up about four feet apart.

To play: At a signal, they race by jumping first to the right, then to the left, then straight ahead. First to finish wins. Or require them to cross the finish line and return. Try playing a record and having them jump to music.

What makes it click: Peer competition. Physical skill. Humor. Rhythm.

Up and Down Stairs   ALL

Have steps or stairs available, or seat the children in rows, to imitate stairs. Provide a pebble, button, penny or other small object.

To play: Players all sit on the lowest step. "It" holds the pebble in one of his hands, fists closed so that no one can tell which hand holds the pebble. He moves his fists alternately up and down from the elbow, chanting "Up and down stairs," holding his fists in position when the chant ends. The first player in the step line then guesses whether the pebble is in the up or the down fist. If he guesses right, he moves up to the second step. "It" starts his fist movements again after rehiding the pebble, and player # 2 gets to guess. Anyone missing stays where he is. Anyone guessing correctly moves up one step. The game goes on through the first line, then to the players who have moved to the second step, etc. The first player to reach the top step becomes "it," and the former "it" takes a seat at the end of the first step.

What makes it click: Element of chance. Peer competition. Concentration.

Wrap It Up   SO, AT

Provide a ball of cord or twine for each team.

To play: Children form two teams, each lining up behind a captain. At a signal, player # 1 holds onto the end of the cord, and passes the ball to player # 2, and so on to the end of the line, where it starts back up the line on the other side of the team, thus circling the team. So on until the ball of cord is all used up, and the team is all wrapped up. First team to finish wins. Replay, winding the cord into a ball as it is passed along, and you'll get your cord back in usable condition, as well as make an exciting game.

What makes it click: Novelty. Team competition. Agility.

Auto Tag   VY, SO

Provide a blindfold of cloth or use a paper bag instead.

To play: The children scatter around "it," who is blindfolded. One child calls out, "How many cars in your garage?" "It" answers "Two." "What colors are they?" "Red and grey." "Turn around twice and tag who you may." At that, no player may move more than two steps in any direction, and "it" tries to catch somebody. When he does, he must identify that person. If he succeeds, that person becomes the new "it."

What makes it click: Drama. Peer competition. Suspense.

Back Up   ALL

Play a record or sing a song with a strong beat.

To play: One player is "it," and announces the type of movement that must be done to the music, such as hopping, skipping, twisting, etc. (if played with older children, use the latest dances popular with the teens). When the music stops, everybody must dash to try to get back to back with somebody. The person left out, or the last two to get together become the next "it."

What makes it click: Boy-girl appeal. Concentration. Novelty.

Hare and Tortoise Race   VY, SO

Get the players into relay teams of equal number, lined up behind a starting line and facing a goal line about thirty feet away (less if played indoors or in a smaller outdoor area).

To play: At a signal, player # 1 on each team must run to the goal line and back, touching # 2. Player # 2 must walk to the goal line and back, touching # 3. Player # 3 runs, player # 4 walks, and so on. The first team to get all its players back in place wins.

What makes it click: Team spirit. Peer competition. Physical speed. Following rules.

Husky Race   SO

This is a good game for boys. Provide several sturdy cardboard boxes big enough for a boy to sit in. Each should have a strong rope attached to it for pulling. Mark a starting and finish line.

To play: Divide the boys into teams of six players, one to be the Eskimo who sits in his sled and drives his five Huskies. The Huskies pull in groups of two, with the head Husky in front. At the signal, the dog sleds are off and running. First to get to finish line, over it and back to starting line wins. If a sled overturns, the Eskimo must right it and get in before he can resume race.

What makes it click: Cooperative action. Peer competition. Excitement. Danger of spills.

Indians   VY

Get the children's attention. Perhaps give them all an Indian headdress (brown paper head band with a real or cardboard feather in the front).

To play: Everybody bends his body forward, tiptoes around, looking to the right and to the left, with hands above eyes. Move into a circle in the middle of the room or on the playing area. Do a war dance. Join hands and go to the center of the circle and back again. End the dance with a war whoop.

What makes it click: Dramatic action. Peer cooperation.

Leg Ball   SO, AT

Materials needed: A volleyball or similar ball. A stick or chalk to mark distance. Ball of string to measure.

To play: Boys line up backwards behind a starting line. They take turns throwing the ball from between their legs. The one with the longest distance wins. Or give each boy three tries, letting him keep his best record.

What makes it click: Peer and self-competition. Physical skill. Humor.

Lions and Tigers   SO

Find a piece of cardboard; crayon black stripes on one side of it, solid yellow on the other side. The striped side represents a Tiger, the plain side a Lion. Or draw the animals if you're good at drawing. Or glue cut-outs to the cardboard.

Divide the youngsters into two groups, the Lions and the Tigers. Leave a space between them.

To play: You're the Ringmaster, and stand in the open space between the Lions and the Tigers. Parade around the room or play area first, everybody imitating the animals. Then throw the cardboard into the air. When it comes down with the stripes on top, the Tigers must all whistle. If the plain side comes on top, the Lions must all roar. If any animal makes a mistake, he must sit down on the sideline. Player who stays in the game the longest wins, or the team with the most players left after a given playing time.

What makes it click: Quick reaction and observation. Team competition. Suspense. Drama.

Magic Carpet   VY, SO

Mark several circles on the floor (masking tape can be removed easily). Or use poster paint or chalk (it will wash off readily). These are Magic Carpets.

To play: Appoint one child to be the leader, or be the leader yourself. Everyone joins hands, and skips, or runs, or hops in, through, and around the Magic Carpets, doing whatever the leader does. When music stops, or a whistle blows, everybody must stop still. All those inside or touching a circle must sit down along the wall, out of the way. Continue until only one player is left. He becomes the next leader.

What makes it click: Suspense. Imitative action. Delightful apprehension. Dramatic action.

Mickey Mouse   VY, SO

Get the children into a circle. That's the mousetrap. Number them off by threes. Appoint Mickey Mouse. Place a ball, beanbag or other object in the center of the circle to represent the cheese.

To play: Mickey Mouse calls for Ones, Twos or Threes. If he yells "Ones," each player with that number must leave his place, run around the circle on the outside, come back to his place, run through it and try to pick up the cheese before any of the other Ones. The first to do this is the new Mickey Mouse.

What makes it click: Anticipation. Physical skill. Competition. Suspense. Quick reaction to command.

Breathe Deep (Tillicum, Tillicum)   SO, AT

A good Indian game new to most players. Provide twenty small objects, such as pebbles, nuts, washers, or anything not too round. Draw two lines about three feet apart (closer for shorter-arm children).

To play: Each player sits between the two lines, ten of the pebbles about three inches apart on one of the lines, the other ten on the other line. At the signal "On your mark," each player takes a deep breath. At the word "Go," each player tries to see how many pebbles he can move from one side to the other, one to the right, one to the left, etc., while he says "Tillicum, tillicum" over and over again while exhaling. He must not inhale. Other players act as judges, and count the number of "tillicums," or the number of transfers of pebbles he has made. Best record wins.

What makes it click: Peer and self-competition. Agility.

Chopstick Relay   so, at

Provide a balloon and two sticks (chopsticks are fine) per team.

To play: Players line up in equal teams, behind a starting line and facing a goal line, post, or wall. Player # 1 on each team has a balloon and the chopsticks. At the signal, he must hold the balloon between the sticks, run to the goal and back, and transfer the balloon and sticks to player # 2, neither of them touching the balloon with his hands. If the balloon is dropped, it must be picked up with the sticks. So on, until every player on a team has had his turn, and the line is back in its original order. First team to do so wins. Try best two out of three.

What makes it click: Novelty. Humor. Team spirit.

Hunter   vy, so

Appoint one child to be the Hunter.

To play: Everyone selects a safety spot in the room or playing area. It may be a post, wall, chair, tree, or a circle drawn on the floor or ground. Each child stands on or touching his safety spot as the Hunter runs around the area, going from person to person, saying "Come hunt with me." As he says this to a player, that player must get in line behind the Hunter. The game goes on until everyone is in the line, and the Hunter has led them away from their safety spots. Finally, the hunter yells "Bang!" At that, everybody, including the Hunter, dashes for a safety spot. The player left out, without a safety spot, becomes the next Hunter.

What makes it click: Suspense. Drama. Peer competition.

Kangaroo Hop   SO, AT

A bit like Squeeze It, but more difficult, and played by teams, not individuals. Provide a volleyball or other fairly soft ball per team.

To play: Teams line up behind a captain, who has the ball. At a signal, he passes the ball over his head to the player behind him, and so on until the ball reaches the last person. He must place the ball between his knees, put his hands on his hips, and hop to the front of the line. When there, he passes the ball over his head, etc. First team to get its players back into original formation wins. If ball is dropped, or player takes hands from hips, he must return to that place before resuming.

What makes it click: Excitement. Humor. Team spirit.

Circle Right   SO

Get the youngsters into two or more circles of equal number. Eight or ten to a circle is a good number. Appoint a captain for each team.

To play: The players stand about a step apart, facing clockwise. At the signal, the captain of each circle runs forward around the circle, back to his place, and taps the shoulder of the player in front of him. That player dashes around the circle, returns to his place, tapping the player in front of *him.* So on, until each player has had his turn, and the last player has tapped the captain's shoulder. The captain then raises his hands high. First to do so is the winning team.

What makes it click: Team competition. Team spirit. Physical skill.

Feather Blow   SO, AT

Materials needed: A sheet and a fluffy feather.

To play: The children hold the sheet as taut as possible, and neck-high. Then each blows, trying to keep the feather from coming his way and touching him. If it does, he is "out."

Variation: For older, more aggressive children, use a ping-pong ball and a blanket in place of the feather and the sheet. It is not easy to keep the blanket taut, keep the ball from rolling off, or from touching the player, especially when players start giggling.

What makes it click: Novelty. Humor. Quick reactions.

Pass It   SO, AT

Assemble two big baskets or boxes full of the same number of odds and ends. Include items of different sizes, shapes, colors, textures and weights, such as books, balls, clothespins, paper clips, spools, pencils, spoons, thimbles, tin pans, old envelopes, and the like. Provide two other empty boxes or baskets. Appoint two captains to choose two teams.

To play: Captains choose players, who get into lines behind their captains. One of the filled baskets or boxes is placed in front of each captain, and an empty one in front of the last player on each team. At a signal, each captain takes one item out of the basket and starts it going down the line to the last player, who puts it into the empty basket. If an item is dropped, it must be taken up to the captain to start it over again. The team that gets all the items into the empty basket first is the winner. Try two times out of three.

What makes it click: Team spirit. Excitement of competition. Agility of movement.

Penny Pitching   SO, AT

Materials needed: Five bright pennies for each child. Foil, paper or tin pie plate for every two children.

To play: Youngsters form two equal lines, facing each other about ten feet apart (vary the distance to suit the ages of the players, about half that distance for the younger children). Each player in one line holds a pie plate steady and level, while the child facing him tries to toss his pennies, one at a time, into the plate. He keeps count of the number of pennies that stay in the plate. When all in one line have finished tossing their pennies, they take the plates and hold them while the other line tries its skill in tossing. Play two out of three trials if the children are still eager—and they're likely to be. Players get their five pennies to keep. Or collect the pennies afterwards and use for another penny game.

What makes it click: Competition. Try of skill. Child interest in money.

Pig Push   SO, AT

Stretch two tapes out across the floor or ground, keeping them about three feet apart. Provide two bright pennies.

To play: Select two boys for each race. Each must push a penny to the end of the tape, using only his nose! Winners of each race compete for final victory.

What makes it click: Humor. Physical agility. Peer competition.

Pillow Play   SO, AT

Provide a sofa pillow (not one of your best) and a carpeted or grassy area because there'll be spills. Get the youngsters into a circle around the pillow, name half the circle Blues, the other half Reds.

To play: The youngsters join hands and dance around the pillow. At a signal, the Blues and Reds try to pull and tug until somebody touches the pillow. That player drops out. The game continues until only one Blue and one Red are left circling around the pillow, then until one succeeds in making the other touch the pillow.

Variations: Use holiday or other symbols for team names, such as Bunnies and Chicks, Witches and Goblins, Cowboys and Indians, and the like. When played outdoors, substitute a bean-bag, a tin pie plate, block of wood, or other flat object for the pillow. The game can be played without teams, everyone for himself.

What makes it click: Competition. Suspense. Agility. Element of aggression.

Pin the Tail on the Donkey   VY

(Yes, it's old as the hills, but did you ever know a more versatile game, or one more universally popular with young children? It's new to them!)

Materials needed: Cloth or paper on which the donkey or other object is drawn or outlined. Blindfold of cloth or paper bag for each child in turn. Yarn or paper "tail" or other item to be pinned or tacked on the object.

To play: Youngsters take turns being blindfolded, turned around, and told to "pin the tail on the donkey."

Substitutes: Pin the button on the clown, the star on the Christmas tree, the hat on the witch, the whiskers on the cat, the ears or tail on the bunny.

What makes it click: Suspense. Slight element of fear. Child humor.

Ring Around   VY, SO

Thread a ring or button on a long piece of twine or cord. Tie the end together, making the knot as small as possible. Get the youngsters together into a circle, standing or sitting, each player holding his hands loosely on the twine.

To play: The youngsters choose one player to be "it." He or she stands in the center of the circle and watches the others. They try to pass the ring along the string to each other, keeping it hidden, and trying not to show who has it by any facial expression. "It" tries to guess. If correct, the person whose hands covered the ring, or were the last to touch the ring, is the new "it."

What makes it click: Suspense. Dramatic action.

Spider   SO, AT

Provide a sharp-pointed stick, Indian club, bowling pin, beanbag or other object. Set a safety zone—a tree, side of the house, or other area.

To play: Everyone joins hands in a circle around the stake or other object in the center of the ring. (If stake is used, drive it into the ground.) At a signal, the circle begins to move, everybody pulling and pushing, trying to make somebody touch the stake. When this happens, that person becomes the Spider. The circle disbands, and the Spider tries to tag as many of the others as he can before they reach the safety zone. This game is similar to Pillow Play, but with a tag game added. Use the former for the older children, this one for the younger.

What makes it click: Peer competition. Legitimate roughhouse. Excitement of the chase.

Squirrel and Nut   VY

Provide a nut or other small object. Get the youngsters into a circle. Appoint one player to be Squirrel.

To play: Each child holds out his right hand, but keeps his head down and eyes shut. Squirrel goes around, pretending to drop the nut into various hands. Finally he *does* drop the nut into a hand, and then runs. The player with the nut must chase the Squirrel and try to catch him before Squirrel gets back to the vacant place in the circle.

What makes it click: Anticipation. Suspense. Peer competition in running.

String Hunt   ALL

Cut a ball of string into various lengths, from two feet to two inches. Hide the strings all over the playing area.

To play: At a signal, the players start hunting and collecting as many of the strings as possible. When everyone has had time to search, signal for the end of the hunt. Each youngster must place his strings, end to end, along the floor or ground. The winner is the one with the longest *line*, not the most strings. Second prize goes to the player with the most strings.

What makes it click: Surprise. Suspense. Observation. Mild competition.

Zoo Race   VY, SO

Mark off a starting line, and a goal line about thirty feet away (shorter if the youngsters are very young, or the space limited). Line the children up in relay teams behind the starting line. Give the same animal names to the first, second, third, etc. players on each team. For example, player # 1 on each team is a Lion; each player # 2 is a Dog; each # 3 is a Duck, etc.

To play: At the signal, each player # 1 (Lion) must race and roar to the goal line, run back, and touch # 2. Number 2 (Dog) must race barking all the way and back, touching #3, the Duck. Duck must waddle and quack, and so on, until each player has raced and pantomimed his animal, and the team is back in place. First team to get all the players back in place wins.

What makes it click: Humor. Competition. Pantomime. Team cooperation.

Caterpillar Race   SO, AT

Provide a strip of cloth about two feet long, or a piece of soft rope, one per team of two players.

To play: Two boys on a team, one kneeling, fingertips on a starting line. The other kneels, too, but facing the opposite way. The cloth is used to tie one ankle of each boy to the other's. At a signal the human caterpillars race to the goal line. The "head" of the caterpillar touches this line, yells "Back!" and his partner starts back to the starting line, thus becoming the caterpillar's head. The first caterpillar to get back behind the starting line wins. Play best two out of three. Then tie *both* ankles of both boys to those of each other. A new, harder race!

What makes it click: Humor. Team spirit. Agility.

Lollipop Hunt   VY

Provide a blindfold of cloth or paper bag for each player. Scatter a dozen or so lollipops inside a large circle.

To play: Children form a circle, facing outward, and are blindfolded. At a signal, they get on their hands and knees and crawl *backwards* into the circle, groping to find any of the lollipops. If the children are wearing heavy shoes, they should remove them before this game. Finders keepers for the lollipops.

What makes it click: Element of luck. Novelty. Reward.

Ten Little Indians   VY

Remember or learn the tune to the old song. Provide Indian headbands and feathers, or ankle bells if you want to dress this game up.

To play: Everybody sits in a circle. You sit in the center, clapping your hands or tapping a drum to mark the time. Number the children off from one through ten. As each number is called in the song (One little, two little, three little Indians, etc.), that child must jump up, keep on singing, and Indian dance around the circle. When everyone is up and dancing, and the song reaches its peak, give a big clap and the children all give a war whoop. Then *reverse* the order (Ten little, nine little, eight little Indians, etc.). Each youngster must go quietly back to his place, sit down and sing softly. Play several times. Young children love it.

What makes it click: Rhythm. Drama. Pantomime.

Wind Tunnel   SO

Get the youngsters into a double circle, partners facing each other with arms joined, forming an arch.

To play: Appoint "it." "It" walks around the circle, finally tapping the shoulder of some player and taking that player's place in the circle. The tapped player and his partner drop hands, the outside player turning right, the inside player turning left, and they both dash under the arched hands that make the tunnel. Each tries to get back to the one empty space. The loser becomes "it" in the next round. For a number of players, or if the game drags on, use several "it"s.

What makes it click: Peer competition. Quick reactions.

Bag Bango   ALL

Materials needed: A paper bag, one-pound size, for each child. Wastebasket for the litter.

To play: Divide the youngsters into two teams, each lined up behind a captain, and facing a table, chair or goal line about ten or fifteen feet away. Place the bags in two equal piles on the table, chair or goal line. At the signal, player # 1 runs to his pile, picks up one bag, blows it up and bursts it with as loud a bang as possible. He then runs back, touches player # 2, and goes to the end of his line. Player # 2 runs to get his bag, blows it up, bursts it, runs back and touches player # 3. So on, until the team has burst all its bags and is back in its original line. First team to do this is the winner.

What makes it click: Aggression. Team spirit. Suspense.

Cat and Rat   VY

Get the youngsters into a circle. Appoint a Cat and a Rat.

To play: The Rat is inside the circle of joined hands, the Cat outside. Cat says, "I am the Cat." Rat answers, "I am the Rat." Cat says, "I'll catch you!" Rat replies, "No, you won't." Then the chase begins.

Both Cat and Rat can go in and out of the circle. The players favor Rat, however, and raise their arms to let him go in and out. Cat, poor thing, must *force* his way in and out. When Rat is caught, he joins the circle, Cat becomes Rat, and a new Cat is chosen. Play dramatically, with lots of squeaks and meows.

What makes it click: Drama. Agility. Suspense. Competition.

Hot Potato   SO, AT

A fine game known by many names, and easily adapted to any age group. Get the youngsters into a circle, sitting on the floor or ground. Provide some lightweight object for the "hot potato"; a knotted handkerchief or dishcloth makes a good one. A ball can be used but isn't as much fun.

To play: Somebody is "it," and sits in the middle of the circle, blindfolded, with a whistle to blow. A hand clap can be used, but is not as easy to hear. At the signal, the players pass the hot potato rapidly around the circle. Every now and then "it" blows his whistle. The person holding the hot potato or touching it last, must leave the circle and join "it" in the center. The game goes on until only two players are left to toss it back and forth and one of them is caught by the whistle.

Variation: Instead of "it" and a whistle, use a record and someone to stop it at odd intervals. This is a good indoor version.

What makes it click: Excitement. Suspense. Element of chance.

Name Ball   SO, AT

Provide a fairly large ball (a beach or volleyball is good).

To play: Youngsters form a circle with "it" in the center. "It" throws the ball into the air, at the same time calling the name of one of the players. That player must dash into the circle and try to catch the ball. If he succeeds, he becomes the next "it." If not, he goes back to his place, and "it" throws again.

What makes it click: Suspense. Quick reactions.

Penny Relay   SO

Provide ten pennies per team. Ten players make a good-sized team. There is a chair at each end of each team; in other words, two chairs (or boxes) per team.

To play: Divide the children into two teams, standing in straight lines facing each other. Place ten pennies on the chair or box at the head of each team. Starting with player # 2 every other person in each line holds his hand out, palm up. (This means players 4, 6, 8, etc.)

At the signal, player # 1 on each team picks up one penny from the chair or box, and puts it into the palm of player # 2.

Player # 3 takes it out of # 2's palm and gives it to the palm of # 4. Player # 5 takes it from # 4, and puts it into the palm of # 6, etc. When the penny gets to the last player in the line, he puts it on the chair by him.

The moment the first penny is started, player # 1 starts the second penny down the line in the same manner, and so on, until all ten pennies have been placed in the pile on the chair at the end of the line. The minute that happens, the end player picks up one penny, and starts it back toward player # 1, then the other pennies, just as before. The first team to get all ten pennies back on the chair at the top of the line is the winner.

What makes it click: Team spirit. Suspense. Following rules.

Steps   ALL

Sometimes called Statues, and one of the very best games. Select a post, wall, tree, or other goal. Draw a starting line fifteen or twenty feet from the goal.

To play: One player is "it." He stands at the goal, his back to the others, who all line up on the starting line. As "it" counts to ten, as slowly or as fast as he likes, the others each advance as far and as stealthily as they think wise. When he says "Ten," he turns around quickly. "It" waves anyone he catches in motion when he turns around back to the starting line. The game continues until the players have advanced very close to "it." Then as "it" counts, one of the players tags him, and they all dash back to the safety of the starting line, "it" in hot pursuit. The player tagged by "it" becomes the new "it" in the next round.

What makes it click: Drama. Excitement. Suspense.

Ziggety Zag   SO

Get the children into two circles, each player about five feet from the others. Appoint a captain for each team.

To play: Use this game with Circle Right. They have the same formation, but this is the more difficult. At the signal, each captain must zigzag around the circle, going behind one player, in front of the next, etc., until he gets back to his place. He then taps the player in front of him, who does the same, and so on until everyone has zigzagged and returned. The last player taps the captain, who raises his arms and yells "Ziggety-zag." First to do so wins.

What makes it click: Agility. Team spirit. Following rules.

Kick Up   SO, AT

Provide a lightweight ball, such as a beach ball or a balloon.

To play: Boys lie in a circle on the floor or ground, their feet toward the center. Toss the ball to their feet. They must keep it in the air, using feet only. For larger group, divide youngsters into two teams. Play for three to five minutes. Teams lose a point every time the ball touches the floor. Team with fewest lost points wins.

What makes it click: Agility. Novelty. Competition.

Zoom, Zoom, Eek   VY, SO

Get the children into a circle—and get out of the way!

To play: The circle is an airplane. Everyone runs around in the circle saying "Zoom! Zoom!" Finally, when a player decides to land, he calls out "Eek!" Then everyone must turn and start to zoom in the opposite direction, until someone else says "Eek!" Play until the game gets too noisy.

What makes it click: Drama. Suspense. Outlet for energy.

9

Settle-down Games

or *"What Can We Do NOW?"*

These are the taper-off games, the catch-your-breath games, the change-of-pacers. They'll be useful when the party starts to get boisterous, or when the youngsters begin to get tired. They're fine ways to quiet down before or after eating, and to close the party. Also, they're fine games to play for any reason!

Animals in the Zoo VY

Remember the tune of "Mulberry Bush." Get the youngsters into a circle, each child imitating the animals as they are named in the song.

To play: Sing the words and act out the animals to the tune of "Mulberry Bush." Children circle and sing:

Look at the animals in the zoo, in the zoo, in the zoo.
And all the funny things they do, and we can do them too!
Verses
1. The elephant walks and swings his trunk, swings his trunk, swings his trunk. The elephant walks and swings his trunk, and we can do it, too.
2. The eagle flaps his great big wings, . . .

3. See how the snake goes twisting about, . . .
4. The big hippopotamus winks and blinks, . . .
5. The tall giraffe can stretch his neck, . . .
6. The kangaroo goes jumping about, . . .
7. Camels can march like soldier men, . . .
8. Each little mouse can tiptoe away, . . . (Here each child tiptoes back to his place.)

What makes it click: Drama. Pantomime. Humor. Music.

Blast Off   VY, SO

Provide a mailing tube, some marbles, and a pan, box or waste basket. Set the pan, box or waste basket about five feet beyond a starting line.

To play: The youngsters take turns putting one marble at a time into the tube, holding the tube waist high, and then trying to throw the marble out of the tube into the receptacle. Ten tries each, and highest score wins. Try using ping-pong balls instead of marbles. Increase distance for older children.

What makes it click: Peer and self-competition. Physical skill.

Cats on the Back Fence   SO, AT

Thumbtack tape or use masking tape in two parallel lines along the floor. Divide the youngsters into two groups, perhaps boys versus girls, or each team with boy-girl-boy-girl arrangement.

To play: At a signal, a Cat from each team begins walking backwards down one of the fences, going as fast as possible and meowing all the way. When he gets to the end, he must turn around and come back again. Any Cat that falls off the "fence" must come back and start all over. When a Cat gets back safely, he touches the paw of the next Cat on his team, and that Cat starts off. First team of Cats to walk the fence safely and get back in line wins.

Black cat masks will add more drama to this exciting relay. Or give each Cat a long tail made of a stocking stuffed with newspaper.

What makes it click: Team cooperation. Peer competition. Agility. Suspense. Excitement. Pantomime.

Crazy Answers   SO, AT

Ask each youngster to name one article that will be useful in the kitchen, a different article for each. Then ask questions, and the youngsters have to answer each by giving the name of that article.

To play: Ask all sorts of questions that will turn out to be child-funny:

"Tom, what will you take to school tomorrow?" Tom has to answer by naming the kitchen article that he thought of. "A bread board."

"Dave, where will you sleep tonight?"

"In the dishwasher."

"What have you got in your pocket, John?"

"A refrigerator."

And so on, each child getting his turn, while the others get more and more hilarious.

What makes it click: Children's developing sense of humor. Communication through laughter.

Dog and Rabbit   SO

Get the youngsters into a circle, everyone sitting on the floor or ground. Provide two objects, such as beanbags, stuffed toys, or balls.

To play: Start the first object, representing Rabbit, around the circle, passing from hand to hand. Then start the second object, representing Dog, passing from hand to hand. Can Dog catch Rabbit? Or will Rabbit go around the circle three times and not be caught? Vary by starting Rabbit around clockwise, Dog around counterclockwise. Which will get back to you first?

What makes it click: Physical agility. Drama. Suspense.

Hul Gul   so

Give each player a bag of twelve beans. (Peanuts will work, but the players probably will eat them!) Get the youngsters into a circle or a line.

To play: Player # 1 puts his hand into his bag and takes out any number of beans, keeping them locked in his fist. He turns to the player on his left and says, "Hul Gul! Hands full. How many?" Player # 2 guesses. If his guess is fewer, he must make up the difference. If more, Player # 1 must give # 2 the difference. For example, if # 1 holds five beans, and # 2 guesses four beans, # 2 must give # 1 a bean. But if # 2 guesses six beans, # 1 must give a bean to # 2. Player # 2 then turns to # 3, and the game continues until everyone has had two or three chances. Then each player counts his beans, and the one with the most is the winner.

Substitutes: Pennies, buttons, acorns, or holiday symbols such as small candy hearts, black cat cut-outs, candy eggs, and the like. The younger the children, the fewer the "pieces," so that the arithmetic won't be too difficult.

What makes it click: Suspense. Excitement of winning or losing. Fun of using arithmetic.

Feed the Spider   so, at

Provide a supply of markers in two colors—checkers, pebbles, nuts, bright and dull pennies, etc.—so that each player gets one. Mark off a big spider web on the floor, ground, tennis court, or large piece of paper. Mark values in each area of the web, the smaller the area, the larger the point value.

To play: Divide the youngsters into two equal teams, and give each a colored marker. Teams take turns tossing the markers one by one into the web, trying to make them land in the most valuable areas. When everyone has tossed his marker, the teams count their point values. Play best two out of three.

What makes it click: Element of chance. Novelty.

Snip   SO, AT

Get the players into a circle, seated on chairs or on the ground or floor.

To play: One person starts by standing in the middle of the circle, and spelling some short word, such as "dog." He then points to any other player in the circle, and starts to count to twelve. The person pointed to must quickly name an object starting with each of the letters used in the spelling, for example, doughnut, onion, grape. If he cannot think of a word, or takes too long, he becomes the next "it." For young children, keep the words very simple. The almost-teens can use words of more than three letters after a little practice.

What makes it click: Concentration. Suspense. Challenge.

Jack in the Box   VY

Get the children scattered around the room or in the outdoor play area, and in a stooping position. Appoint a child to be Jack.

To play: Jack stands where everyone can see and hear him. If he claps his hands once, all the boys must jump up; twice, all the girls must jump up; three times, everybody must spring up. Anybody who makes a mistake must get out of the game and come stand by Jack. If the game goes well, play until only one person is left. He or she becomes the next Jack. If the action is slow, or the game seems to be taking too long, appoint a new Jack frequently, so as to give everyone a chance to be the clapper.

What makes it click: Importance of paying attention and following orders. Peer competition. Suspense.

Old Hen and Chickens   VY

Choose a child to be the Old Hen, and send her out of the room, or behind a door, or somewhere out of sight. The other youngsters all sit with their heads bowed. Silently, touch four of

them on the head. They are the chicks. Then call Mother Hen
back into the room.

To play: Mother Hen says "Cluck, cluck," and the four chicks
must answer "Peep, peep," but not raise their heads. Mother
Hen tries to locate them by sound. The Chick discovered first
becomes the Old Hen for the next game.

What makes it click: Suspense. Drama. Imitative action.
Humor.

Penny Drop   SO, AT

Find a large, wide-mouthed glass jar, old fishbowl, or other
fairly wide and deep holder. It must be large enough to hold a
small glass, such as used for fruit juice or jelly. Fill the big
container with water and sink the small glass in the middle of
the bottom.

To play: Each child gets five bright pennies, and in turn, tries
to drop his pennies, one at a time, into the small glass. Keep a
record, and run play-offs with the children who have the best
scores. Final winner gets all the pennies outside the small glass.
Runner-up gets those inside the small glass. Or give another type
of award and use those pennies for other penny games.

What makes it click: Suspense. Peer competition. Hand and
eye coordination.

Picture You!   SO, AT

Collect and cut out, ahead of time, lots of colored pictures of
people used in ads in magazines. Cut off the heads. Mount the
bodies on cardboard to give them greater durability. Same with
the heads. Or cut the heads off photographs of friends, family or
famous people that the youngsters will recognize.

To play: Mix all the bodies and heads in a big box or basket.
Each youngster draws a body and head. Who makes the funniest
combination? Each child pastes a head to a body, and uses the
finished cut-out as a place card or favor. If family photos are
used, collect and mount for future enjoyment. Imagine Gramp's

head on a ballet dancer's body! Or Junior's face under the headdress of the Queen's Guards. Or Dad's head above a baby's rompers!

What makes it click: Humor. Suspense.

Pumpkin Fortunes II   SO, AT

Provide a real or imitation pumpkin, or other large object, such as a watermelon, or even a large circle of cardboard. On the top of the object, write all the letters of the alphabet, in any sort of order, on small slips of paper and pin them to the object.

To play: Each child in turn is blindfolded, and must stab the object gently with a large pin or other sharp object, until he has stabbed three letters. These are his fortune.

The first letter indicates the name of his or her future wife or husband. The second represents what he will do for a living. The third indicates the kind of person the child will become.

An adult dressed as a gypsy fortune teller should interpret the fortune. For example, the letters drawn might be C, D and H. The fortune teller can pretend to look into her crystal ball, and say: "I see a blonde girl. Her name is Clara—no, I see *Carol*. She is wearing a wedding dress. I see a sign outside your house. What can it be? Oh, I see now, it's *Doctor* William Jones. And I see a word beginning with H—*what* is it? Now it's clear. It is *happy*. You will become a doctor, marry a girl named Carol and be very happy."

What makes it click: Interest in the future. Drama. Suspense.

Shopping   SO, AT

Select one child to be the Shopper. The others form a circle around him.

To play: The Shopper wanders around the circle, and finally stops in front of some player, saying "I'm going to Chicago [or other city or state]. What shall I buy?" He then counts to ten. In that time, the other player must answer by naming three items that begin with C (the first letter of the city or state), such as corn, car, comb. If he doesn't name the three before the count of ten, he becomes the next Shopper.

What makes it click: Suspense. Quick thinking.

Chinese Fingernails   SO, AT

Materials needed: Five clothespins of the plain wooden type (no springs), per each team.

To play: Players line up into two teams, facing each other. Give the five clothespins to the first player in each line. He must put the clothespins on the fingers of one of his hands. Then player # 2 must remove them, and place them on the fingers of one of *his* hands, and so on down the line. The last player must run up to player # 1 and let him remove the clothespins. First team to finish, wins. This is a very good game for boys versus girls, or for mixed teams.

What makes it click: Humor. Agility. Team spirit.

Foo and Koo   SO, AT

Get the youngsters into a big circle.

To play: This game is like the old game of Buzz, but faster and easier. Instead of the number "two," a player must say "foo"; instead of "four," he must say "koo." Fourteen would be one koo; 22 would be foo foo; 24 would be foo koo. One player starts the numbering. Anyone making a mistake must go into the center of the circle, and perhaps later on pay some sort of forfeit. A good game to follow Chinese Fingernails.

What makes it click: Concentration. Humor. Novelty.

Bumble Bee Buzz   ALL

Get the children into two lines, standing back to back, about a foot apart.

To play: At the signal, each player takes a de-e-p breath, turns around and faces his opponent, buzzing like a bee. No one must take a breath; the buzz is made while expelling the breath only.

The bee that buzzes the longest wins. Anyone who laughs must drop out. In case of a tie, conduct a play-off of the players who have buzzed the longest. Play the game several times, because it is happy-making.

Variation: Use as a stunt, with only two players. Then let the others challenge the winner until the King or Queen Bee is decided.

What makes it click: Humor. Pantomime. Competition.

Bottlecap Toss   SO, AT

Provide a good supply of bottlecaps. Mark a throwing line. Place an extra bottlecap any given distance in front of this line.

To play: The youngsters line up behind the starting line, each with a bottlecap. The first player in the line tries to toss his bottlecap into the air in such a way that it will fall and hit the target cap. If he misses, he goes to the end of the line, and player # 2 tries. If his bottlecap hits the target cap, he gets to keep both caps (or all that are in the target area), and you replace the target cap. Play until everyone has had one or several turns, because this is a very absorbing contest. Player with the most caps is the winner.

Variation: Use pennies instead of bottlecaps, or other small objects.

What makes it click: Peer competition. Novelty.

Clap Happy   ALL

Make sure you remember the tune, "She'll Be Coming Round the Mountain."

To play: Sing it right after the refreshments, or just before leaving for home. It creates a nice mood. Everyone sits around informally, or gathers around the piano, sings these words, and follows your movements.

If you're happy and you know it,
Clap your hands (clap, clap) .
If you're happy and you know it,

Clap your hands (clap, clap).
If you're happy and you know it,
Then it's time for you to show it;
If you're happy and you know it,
Clap your hands (clap, clap).

Repeat the song, changing the actions to these:

2. Nod your head (nod, nod).
3. Stamp your foot (stamp, stamp).
4. Do all three (clap, clap, nod, nod, stamp, stamp).

What makes it click: Rhythm. Humor. Action

Donkey and Fiddler   VY

Get the children into a circle.
To play: Appoint "it," who stands in the center and faces any player, while pretending to play a violin. The person he faces must instantly pretend to be a donkey, waving his fingers from his ears. "It" tries to fool the player opposite him by changing rapidly from being the fiddler to the donkey. The person facing him must always react quickly and do the exact opposite. When "it" is the fiddler, the other player is the donkey; when "it" is the donkey, the other must be the fiddler.
What makes it click: Quick reactions. Humor.

Winning Heart   SO, AT

Materials needed: Enough wrapped candy for each player to have five pieces. Cut a heart out of cardboard and crayon or paint it red. Cut an arrow out, too, and color it gold or other color.
To play: Players sit in a circle. One person starts the heart around the circle to the right, and the arrow to the left. You or some other player gives a clap or blows a whistle at odd intervals. At that signal, whoever has the arrow must give whoever has the heart a piece of his candy. The whistle blows again; the game resumes and continues until most of the candy has changed

hands. The person with the most candy in his possession is the winner and gets to keep all of his winnings.

What makes it click: Suspense. Chance. Reward. Novelty.

Variations: Use beans, pebbles, pennies, peanuts or other objects instead of candy. Use other holiday symbols instead of the heart and arrow.

Goose Egg   ALL

A bit similar to Hot Potato, but a quieter game, easy to play on floor or table. Cut out enough cardboard "eggs" to provide one per child. They should all look alike on one side, but one should have the word "goose" crayoned on the other side.

To play: The youngsters sit at a table or on the floor. Place a cardboard egg in front of each. At a signal, each child passes his egg to the right by sliding it along and keeps passing each egg as he receives it from the player on his left. When you call "Stop," they turn their eggs over, and whoever has the goose egg falls out of the game. Remove one of the ordinary eggs, shuffle the others, and distribute them as before. The game goes on, one child and one egg being eliminated at each round, until finally only one child is left. He is the winner.

Variations: Use other holiday symbols to be passed along. Or use a playing card per child, the Joker taking the place of the goose egg, and play as above.

What makes it click: Suspense. Humor. Element of chance.

Ha CHU, Ha CHO   SO

This is a nice variation of the old games, Simon Says, and I Say Stoop. Get the children into a circle, with one child as "it" in the center.

To play: Every time "it" says "Ha CHU" and bows, every child must do the same. If "it" says "Ha CHO," no one must move. "It" tries to catch somebody not alert by varying his words and bows. If he succeeds, that person becomes the new "it." Try to get a lively, alert child to be the first "it," and this game will click at once.

What makes it click: Suspense. Peer competition. Drama.

Hold Your Breath   so, at

Provide one or more bottles, depending upon the size of the group. One bottle to each ten or less players is about right. Each bottle should have a fairly small mouth but be fairly stable. Provide twenty toothpicks per child.

To play: Place the bottle on the table or floor. The youngsters sit or stand around it, each with his pile of toothpicks in front of him. They take turns putting one toothpick at a time across the top of the bottle. If a player's toothpick dislodges any or all of the toothpicks, the player must add all the fallen toothpicks to his pile. The first player to get all his toothpicks used up is the winner.

What makes it click: Tremendous suspense. Tension. Drama. Concentration.

Shocking   so, at

Collect a dozen or so small items, such as a key, coin, matchbox, pencil, spoon, etc.

To play: Send one child out of the room. The others select one of the objects to produce the electric shock. Call the player back and tell him that one of the objects will give him an electric shock when he touches it. He must find out which it is by touching each object with his forefinger and holding it there a second. When the player touches the selected object everyone gives a loud screech, and the player will certainly jump.

What makes it click: Child humor. Suspense. Novelty.

Silent Circle   vy

Get the children into a circle.

To play: One child is "it," and stands in the center of the circle. The others must be absolutely silent. "It" beckons to some child in the circle. That child must walk to the center without making even a tiny noise. If he does go silently, "it" shakes hands with him, and he becomes the new "it." If he does make a sound, "it" shakes his head, won't shake hands, and that player must go back to his place in the circle.

What makes it click: Novelty. Challenge. Suspense.

Catch a Smile   VY, SO

Get the children into a circle.

To play: You start off as the first "it." Smile a BIG smile, look at some child, wipe your smile off with your hand and throw it to that child. He must catch it, put it on, wear it for a moment, then wipe it off and throw it to some other child. Nobody else must smile, and the thrower must not leave even a trace of the smile on his own face.

What makes it click: Novelty. Humor. Following a rule.

Clothespin Fumble   SO, AT

A good game for girls. Tie a cord between the backs of two chairs about six feet apart to represent a clothesline. Provide twelve clothespins (doll-size will do) and a blindfold of cloth or paper bag.

To play: In turn, blindfold each child, and hand her the clothespins, one at a time. She must try to put the clothespins on the line, *using only one hand.* The child getting the most clothespins on the line is the winner. Nice game for a doll party.

What makes it click: Humor. Spectator appeal. Suspense.

Why? Because!   SO, AT

Provide a sheet of paper and pencil for each player. Divide players into two teams, the Whys and the Becauses.

To play: Each person on the Why team writes a question, no matter how silly, on his slip of paper, each question starting off with "Why?" Each player on the Because team writes down some reason, no matter how silly, beginning "Because." Nobody on either side tells anyone else what he has written. Collect all the Why slips, mix them up, and place them in a single pile. Do the same for the Because slips. One at a time, a player from the Why team selects a Why slip, reads it, and a player from the Because team picks out one of the Because slips and reads it in answer.

What makes it click: Humor. Novelty. Suspense.

Word Play   SO, AT

Provide a sheet of paper and a pencil for each guest.

To play: Each person divides his paper into twenty-five squares, five across and five down. Then each in turn calls out any letter of the alphabet, and everybody puts that letter into any of the squares. Once written, it cannot be erased or changed. When all the squares have been filled, the puzzle starts. Each player tries to make as many three-, four- or five-letter words as possible, moving one square at a time up, down, or across. Five-letter words count ten points; four-letter, five points; three-letter, two points. A word that has been counted cannot be broken up. High score wins.

What makes it click: Novelty. Challenge.

Simon Says   VY

A variation of a game played many different ways. This way is very absorbing to young children. Seat the children around a table or on the floor or ground.

To play: Stand or sit where they can all see and hear you. Everyone makes a fist of his right hand, and rests it, thumb side up, on the table, floor or knee. You call for three actions, thumbs up, thumbs down, and wiggle-waggle. The children must imitate your actions whenever you precede your order with "Simon says." For example, if you say, "Simon says—Thumbs up!", everyone must raise his thumb. If you say "Thumbs up!", nobody must move his thumb. Play it fast. Fists must be removed if a mistake is made. The last player left in the game is the winner, and becomes the new Simon.

What makes it click: Novelty. Humor. Suspense. Quick reactions.

Stories—A to Z   SO, AT

Provide a sheet of paper and a pencil for each player.

To play: Each guest must write a story in which each letter of the alphabet is used *in order* to begin each word. In a reasonable time, each person then reads his tale aloud, and the group votes on the best.

What makes it click: Challenge. Novelty.

Laced Up   AT

Select a boy and girl, and provide a pair of sneakers large enough for them. If they are wearing sneakers, they can use their own.

To play: The boy and girl sit side by side with the shoes on their outside feet unlaced three holes down. At a signal, each must lean over and lace up and tie the other's outside shoe, without moving either foot. The first couple to finish is the winner.

Variations: This makes a good spectator stunt, when one or two couples compete and the others watch. It also makes a good forfeit stunt for losers in other contests.

What makes it click: Humor. Boy-girl appeal. Novelty.

Monogram Fortunes   AT

Provide a sheet of paper and a pencil for each player. Work up a set of questions ahead of time.

To play: Each guest writes his or her initials across the top of the paper, then exchanges it with someone else's. As the questions are read out, each person must answer them by using words that begin with the initials on the paper. For example, if the initials were C.R.:

Q: What does the person look like?
A: A crumpled roadmap.
Q: How old is he?
A: Comparatively recent.

When all the questions have been answered, the papers are returned, and each reads his fortune aloud.
What makes it click: Humor. Novelty.

Along Came a Spider   vy

Learn the words, tune and movements of this action song. The children will love it.
To play: Sing the little song first to learn the words.

A long came a spi der and climbed up a spout;

Down came the rain and washed the spi der out.

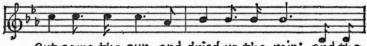
Out came the sun and dried up the rain; and the

lit tle brown spi der climbed up the spout a gain.

Words and Action

Along came a spider (make two fingers walk)
And climbed up a spout; (spiral upward with one hand)
Down came the rain (lower both hands, moving fingers)
And washed the spider out. (draw hands apart)
Out came the sun (point up)
And dried up the rain; (draw hands apart)
And the little brown spider (make fingers walk)
Climbed up the spout again. (spiral upward)

What makes it click: Child humor. Rhythm. Drama.

Telegrams   AT

A good game for girls. Provide an index card, or small sheet of paper, and a pencil for each player, and ask each person to print the name of somebody she likes, such as a movie star, popular singer, writer or favorite boy friend.

To play: Each must write an imaginary telegram to that person, using each letter in the printed name. When all the telegrams have been written, each girl reads hers out loud, or they all exchange cards so that each reads another's telegram.

What makes it click: Conforms to peer interests and fads. Makes for girl-talk. Allows the airing of personal feelings.

Who Are You?   AT

Provide a sheet of tablet or typing paper and a pencil for each player. Prepare a list of about ten questions.

To play: Each player writes an answer to the same question, then folds his answer over, so that the writing is hidden, and passes it to the player on his or her right. This goes on until all the questions have been answered, except the last: "Who Are You?" At this point, each person signs his name. They then read the papers aloud to the group, one person asking the questions. Suggested questions:

My favorite food is _____.
My three pet peeves are _____.
My favorite boy (or girl) friend is _____.
I want to be a _____.
My favorite singer is _____.
What I like to do best is _____.
What I most dislike doing is _____.
I wish I were _____.
I'm glad I'm not _____.
My name is _____.

This game can be adapted to many situations, and used as pure comedy or as a sort of fortune-telling. It is usually popular with the older girls, or with the older boys and girls.

What makes it click: Suspense. Humor. Anticipation.

Witch and the Cat   SO, AT

Pair off the youngsters. Place two straight chairs on opposite sides of the room. Provide two apples or other objects, such as potatoes, blocks, and the like.

To play: One player is the Witch, and the other is the Cat. Each sits in one of the chairs. At a signal, each must put an apple on his head, walk to the other chair and sit down. While seated, the Witch must give a horrible grin, and the Cat must meow mournfully. Each then rises and walks back to his starting chair, apple still on head. Any player dropping the apple is eliminated and must go to the ghosts' corner, out of the way. Play until everyone has had a turn. Then play off the winners until only one Witch and one Cat remain.

Variations: If the children are too skillful, make this game more difficult by allowing the "ghosts" to try to make the couple laugh, or require the couple to get up and sit down three times.

What makes it click: Peer competition. Humor. Pantomime. Suspense.

PART III

≈

RED-LETTER DAYS

or

"But We Want to CELEBRATE!"

This section describes a number of *types* of parties that children enjoy at various ages, along with some ideas and methods for making them successful.

Birthdays are the reddest of all red-letter days, but a red-letter day really doesn't need any excuse or reason. It may be a holiday-in-the-air feeling. It may be an answer to the weather, whether cold or hot. It may be a popular event expected at a certain age, such as a slumber party or a sleep-out.

The child who grows up in a family that enjoys traditions, the seasons, holidays and special days, and turns any event into a happening or an occasion, is a lucky child. He or she is very likely to enjoy living, and the simple pleasures of sharing good times with his own family and friends.

The parties suggested here are basic ideas which provide plenty of opportunity for you to deck them out and add new twists. In some cases, for a very informal party, or for very young children, they will need very little padding. For older youngsters, and for longer-lasting parties, add some of the games from Part II, as few or as many as you need. Select them to fit the ages of the party-comers. Select and plan to use more than you think you'll need. Then, if one doesn't click, you won't be stuck with that horrible feeling of "What do we do now?"

Use the age-level Quick Party-planning Guide to find and select games suitable for use at these parties. The right games for the right group will click!

10

❧⟐❧

Party Plans

 or *"Please Make It SPECIAL!"*

The themes and suggestions for these parties should be used with discretion. Change them. Add or subtract activities to suit *your* party. Apply them to other themes and occasions. But remember that while children beg for the new, they are basically conformists. The old, dressed up a bit, is often what they mean by "new." Novelty can be added by currently popular color schemes, current slang and child-vocabulary, originality in decoration of the house, in favors and in food. Consult the Quick Party-planning Guide for games for the very young, the slightly older and the almost teens.

The Birthday Party   ALL

No holiday or special day, even Christmas, means quite the same as a birthday to a child. In the first place, it is uniquely *his* or *her* own day, an ego-satisfying, personal-identification day, with the spotlight of attention focused at close-up range. In the second place, each birthday is a step toward the ultimate, heavenly teen years, looked upon enviously by the Just-Belows.

The birthday party can be an all-family event, in which the

observance takes on certain family traditions. For example, birthday gifts can appear magically at the breakfast table when the birthday falls on Saturday or Sunday, or during vacation days. Or the gifts can be hidden all over the house, and an impromptu treasure hunt can start or finish the day.

Birthday choice is a popular way to celebrate. The birthday child decides ahead of time upon some special thing he or she would like to see or do, such as a trip to the zoo, a ball game, a children's play or movie, ice skating, dinner at a restaurant, a beach picnic, and the like. Sometimes this becomes a family affair; sometimes he is allowed to invite one or more friends.

In addition to, or in place of, the all-family or family-only birthday party, there comes a time when the child's social instincts demand a wider outlet, and other children are needed to establish the social status of growing up. That's when you'll start planning for the birthday party. The general comments and suggestions in Part I will be helpful in your planning.

The main thing to keep in mind is to *spotlight* the birthday child. This is easy to do, and makes the party a *real* party!

• Provide some sort of special headgear for each guest (funny party hats, cowboy hats, train or sailor caps, crowns, head scarves, bonnets, berets, coolie hats, Island hats), but give the birthday child the biggest, the brightest, or a different kind, so that he or she stands out. The same principle holds in providing any special favor or decoration such as leis, balloons, bracelets, necklaces, sashes, and the like. The birthday child must be identifiable.

• At the lunch, dinner or refreshment table, the birthday child gets the seat at the head of the table. His place should be easy to find, marked with a huge, silver-foil star-shaped place mat, or a place mat of a different color from the others.

• His or her chair can be gilded for the occasion, or a big bunch of balloons attached to it, or a big bow tied at the top, or a crown suspended above it.

• The birthday cake should be paraded around the table, then set down in front of the birthday child. He blows out the candles or gets the first blow. He gets the decorations on it, if he wants them. If cupcakes are used instead of one big cake, his cupcake should have a bigger or different color candle, or several small ones, in contrast with the one-candle, all-alike cupcakes of the other children.

• The birthday child should be given certain concessions in the games, such as being "it" in the first game, or the first player to be blindfolded, or the leader in a game line.

• In case the birthday party goes on a trip or to a drugstore or other place or event where money has to be used, the birthday child should have the fun and privilege of paying the bus, taxi or carfare, and the meal tab or other fee. (It is good training, too, for the future host or hostess.)

Birthday Information

Sometimes, right when you need it most, it is hard to find out information about the birthday flower and birthstone. These are often useful in planning decorations and gifts. Here they are, subject to variation:

Month	Flower	Birthstone
January	carnation	garnet
February	violet	amethyst
March	jonquil	aquamarine
April	sweet pea	diamond
May	lily-of-the-valley	emerald
June	rose	pearl
July	larkspur	ruby
August	gladiola	bloodstone
September	aster	sapphire
October	calendula	opal
November	chrysanthemum	topaz
December	narcissus	turquoise

Circus Party   VY, SO

Popular with the five-through-sevens. Colorful, gay, and can include all sorts of activities. Invitations can have an unblown-up balloon enclosed, or can be printed with poster paint on a big balloon. On the front door, or tied to the porch, trees and shrubs, *lots* of balloons.

For early arrivals, supply lots of theatrical make-up and let each child make his own clown face. Or supply crayons and let each child decorate his boodle bag with some circusy picture of a clown, balloons, animals, etc. Or use games like What Am I? or Balloon Birds. Then, when everyone has arrived, all sorts of active games, such as Follow the Leader, Frog Race, Lions and Tigers, Lollipop Hunt, Ten Little Indians, and Zoo Race. For tapering off, use games like Animals in the Zoo, Blast Off, Catch a Smile, Are You Happy?, etc.

For refreshments, so important with small children, cupcakes with colored icing, animal cookies, ice cream, milk. Take-homes may be balloons, lollipops, cookies, masks, animal crackers, crazy hats, etc.

I-Hate-Boys Party   so

An all-girl party can celebrate a birthday, an award, a holiday, or be just-for-fun. On the whole, it usually requires less in actual game activities but more in preplanning for decorations, favors and food. Girls are often more appreciative of details in decoration, such as flower arrangements, color schemes, table settings and the like. They are also satisfied more easily with imitative activities, such as dressing-up, playing house and school, doll play, paper-doll play and the like. Most children's games are suitable for all-girl groups, but they'll go best if you play along.

As they grow older, an all-girl party flourishes on self-help in preparing the food, and table decorations, informal girl-talk, recordplaying, dancing to favorite records, working on hairdos and the like.

Set out the mixes, the pans and other kitchen equipment, and let the Elevens and Twelves fix their own dinner. Spaghetti and meatballs, macaroni and cheese, cookies, molded jello salads or desserts are all within their ability to make and to enjoy making. To this do-it-yourself group, you might add an extra, such as tickets to a local movie, a swim at the club or city pool, roller or ice skating at a local or nearby skating rink, bowling at the nearest bowling alley, or a trip to the miniature golf course.

Themes (in addition to holiday or special day themes) suitable for all-girl parties might include the following:

doll's day out	paper-doll party
dress-up party	toy circus day
slumber sleep-in	party potluck
junior miss party	queen-for-a-day party
just-us-girls party	

Doll Party   vy, so

If the small girls in your family or neighborhood are in the play-with-dolls stage, celebrate it! Give a doll party.

Invitations might run like this:

> Be a doll.
> Bring your doll
> to
> Elizabeth Green's doll party,
> July 10, from three to five-thirty.

At the doorway or on the porch, a large, stuffed doll, with a sign, "Doll House." Inside, a gold-paper crown for each little Princess, and a smaller gold crown for her doll. Then, a doll welcoming. Dolls' names given, dolls admired. Perhaps a doll beauty contest, with all the dolls placed side by side on the sofa, in chairs, etc. Blue ribbons, of course, for *all* the dolls. Use classifications like these, plus others:

prettiest	largest	smallest
blondest	most dimples	bluest eyes
longest lashes	most curls	sweetest smile
prettiest dress	most lifelike	oldest

After the showing, everybody can get busy making necklaces, bracelets and earrings for herself and her doll out of beads, macaroni, buttons and other odds and ends. Supply the girls with large sheets of tissue paper and see who can devise the best costume for herself and her doll. As a special treat, give each small girl a beauty shop treatment—using lipstick, eyebrow pencil, rouge and the works—for that lovely "grown-up" feeling. Follow with a beauty parade, all in fun.

Then another project: making clothespin dolls, using scraps of cloth, ribbon, yarn, crayons, etc. If you can find a large packing box, set it up, provide lots of odds and ends like matchboxes, spools, scraps of cloth, tile, etc., and let the girls make and furnish a dollhouse for the clothespin dolls. Or use smaller boxes, and each child makes a model room for her doll. Then hold an exhibit.

For refreshments, doll-size cookies, pink lemonade, ice cream— all served on doll-size dishes, on low tables or boxes, with room for dolly to sit beside her owner.

If doll play runs short, add some simple games, such as Who Am I?, Clothespin Fumble, Cat and Rat, and Catch a Smile (see Quick Party-planning Guide).

Slumber Party or Sleep-in   AT

"Can I stay all night with _____?" is a favorite question, especially for girls. The slumber party has been a perennial favorite for almost every generation.

It is a tremendous experience for some youngsters—the first social event that takes and keeps them away from home overnight. It represents a first step toward attending summer camp, visiting out-of-town relatives alone, even going to college. It is a first step, too, in discovering the everyday habits and way of life of other people outside the family. It requires certain adjustments, certain changes of habits. Along with all the noise and giggling, the youngsters discover that people are different, that there are different ways of cooking, eating, cleaning up, talking, even different ways of thinking. They also learn the rudiments of being guests, and being responsible for guests.

From the parents' point of view, the slumber party is a good way to get to know the children's friends in an informal setting. It also is an opportunity for new experiences for the little hostess in making her guests happy and comfortable.

When your girls ask permission to hold a slumber party, say "yes" and set up some ground rules. Decide upon how many, where, how long, and how. For under-sixes, start out with only one little friend; more is overwhelming. Those first overnights are real parties to the child, but just another place at the table for you—no trouble. To the guest, arriving with her little overnight case (sometimes a big suitcase!) it is a *very* special event.

As the youngsters get older, and slumber parties get larger and noisier, the ground rules start:

• Write or telephone the parents of every child to be invited.

• Tell the date and time of coming and going: "Susie hopes that you'll let Jane come to her slumber party on next Friday night. Could she come to dinner that night and stay over until after lunch on Saturday? I'll send her home around three in the afternoon."

• Tell about living arrangements and what to bring: "There'll be ten girls—and you know our house! They'll have to sleep in the playroom (or living room, etc.), so please tell Jane to bring her sleeping bag (or sheet, blanket and pillow) and towel. She'll need her bathrobe and pajamas, bedroom slippers, and toilet articles. In the morning Susie plans to take them all down to the pool, so tell Jane to bring her bathing suit and slacks (or shorts)."

• Reassure the parents: "Don't worry about Jane. I'll see that she gets *some* sleep, and gets reasonably well-fed! And I'll send her home on time. Jim and I will be on hand, and Susie is all set. You know what it'll be like—lots of giggling, raiding the fridge, working on hairdos, girl-talk far into the night—but they're young, and it won't hurt them!"

• Follow up. Make sure that the youngsters follow the plans. It is a very good idea to invite the youngsters for dinner before the slumber party. Besides meeting the whole family, they'll get

an inkling of family habits and routines and settle into them
with less trouble.

Slumber parties take very little activity planning. Table and
board games such as table tennis, Chinese checkers, cards (Hearts
is usually popular) and other current favorites should be on
hand. A recordplayer is usually a must. TV may be helpful.
(Seeing the late show may be a new treat to some of them.)

Food, of course, is a must. Stock the refrigerator and kitchen
table with soft drinks, peanuts, bread, spreads, cookies—and put
away anything you don't want used or devoured.

With the ten-to-twelves, there'll be much talk about the boys.
You can make a big hit by a bit of fortune-telling, as described
below. They'll love it. After that, leave them alone, unless the
noise gets too much. Set a time limit for loud records. Neighbors
need their sleep.

If possible, let them sleep late. Provide eggs, hot chocolate,
pancakes or whatever you like, but lots of it. If the girls have had
any kitchen training, let them fix their own from mixes you set
out, wash dishes and straighten the kitchen afterwards.

After breakfast, they bathe, dress and get their belongings all
packed up. Then to the pool, beach, yard, or wherever they will
spend the next few hours. A picnic lunch out-of-doors, perhaps,
and then home by three o'clock as you promised.

Tea-leaf fortunes make a big pajama-time hit.

The tea must be brewed in a pot large enough to serve each
guest, and of course requires loose tea in it, not tea bags. Each
guest drinks her cup of tea down to the last few drops. She then
must make a wish, repeating it to herself three times. When this
has been done, she must swirl the drops in her cup around from
left to right three times, so as to get the tea leaves up onto the
sides of the cup. She then turns the cup upside down in its
saucer, and gives the cup three twirls from left to right. Then,
and only then, she gives the cup to the fortune-teller, without
looking at it herself, because if she does, the spell will be broken.

The fortune-teller takes the cup, and "reads" it, starting with
the tea formation in the bottom. This represents the past. She

then goes on interpreting any tea leaves along the sides, going spirally, because the rim of the cup represents the present or near future. (For a fascinated group, use three cups each, for the past, present and future) .

Here's how to interpret tea-leaf symbols:

• A long, hard leaf, forked, or with anything that suggests a hat or cane represents a man. A leaf spread so it looks like a skirt or hat represents a woman.

• A figure alone, surrounded by a group of grounds, promises a suitor, sweetheart, new boy friend.

• A kneeling figure means a proposal of marriage. Where it is in relation to the rim determines whether it is in the past, imminent, or in the future.

• A figure alone, with no grounds around it, indicates no marriage in the period indicated by its location in the cup.

• A heart means a happy love affair.

• Two hearts mean marriage.

• Two figures near each other, with no other grounds nearby, mean an engagement.

• Four dots making a square means a love letter. A dot inside it means good news. Many dots outside mean bad news.

• A ring means a happy marriage.

• A cross means unhappiness or disappointment.

• Five dots in a line mean a journey. If lots of dots are at the end of the line, they mean lots of new friends.

• An anchor means success if it is in the bottom of the cup. If at the top, it means love. In the middle, faithfulness.

• A star means happiness. If it has lots of dots around it, it means long life.

• A serpent indicates an enemy.

• A fish means good luck.

• A leaf folded over the top promises something very unpleasant; a clear rim means a happy future.

• Seven dots in a row mean prosperity.

• Dots in a rectangle mean sickness or bad news.

• A triangle or three dots in a group mean the wish is granted.

Here's how to make and tell inkblot fortunes. Provide each guest with a sheet of typing paper; a bottle of ink, or poster paint; pen or brush. Each guest makes a small blot of ink or paint in the center of the paper, then folds it, and presses to spread the blot. The fortune is then read, based on what can be seen or imagined in the blot. Look at the blot from all angles; then base the reading somewhat on the tea-leaf fortunes, or on what you know about the guest.

The Sleep-out   SO, AT

The sleep-out and the slumber party can be planned for either boys or girls. Usually, however, boys prefer the former; girls the latter. Experiments with hair-dos and cosmetics, requiring indoor accessories, don't interest the boys.

Plan the sleep-out for the boys very much the same way as outlined in the slumber party. Decide how many, when, and where. Notify the parents. Set dates and ground rules. Tell what to bring, when to come, when to go, etc.

Dinner or supper can be indoors or outdoors. Presleep-out games and activities can also be indoor or outdoor—darts, Chinese checkers, table tennis, recordplaying, TV, and the like.

It helps to have the following: an outdoor campfire (the charcoal grill will substitute) for cheerfulness and atmosphere; a recordplayer, or better yet, someone to play a guitar, banjo or accordion; singing; dual stunts such as "cock fights"; sleeping bags inside the tent, or out in the open, to settle down into; a cup of hot chocolate as a surprise.

Be prepared for stragglers coming in from the dark or the cold. Be prepared for a major exodus from outdoors in case of a storm or shower. Most of all, be prepared for sun-risers. They'll wake up at daybreak, hungry as young wolves, and descend upon the kitchen. Here again, if they have been kitchen- or camp-trained, provide mixes, eggs, vast quantities of milk and fruit juices. If you're nervous about their cooking ability, you'll have to be on hand, so do try to train your son in breakfast preparation.

After breakfast, clean-up and dress-up, arrange a trip to the pool, beach, park, ball game, or other morning plan. Then a good lunch (hot dogs or hamburgers are the big favorites) and home at the promised time.

Slumber Sleep-in   AT

It is *possible* to give a combination overnight party, with the boys outdoors and the girls indoors, or boys in the playroom and girls in the bedrooms, but don't do it unless you have *lots* of open space, or neighbors who are either deaf or *very* understanding.

If you are brave enough to consent to this sort of overnight, you'll have to be brave enough to supervise it in terms of noise, horseplay, and sleep time. Preteens get noisier and more boisterous as they get tired and sleepy. Parents who are used to lots of children and lots of noise won't be fazed, but if you've never held a combination boy-girl sleep-in, you are in for a new experience!

Snow Bunny Party   ALL

Wait for the weatherman to cooperate, unless you live in snow country. This party can be almost spur-of-the-minute! The youngsters are underfoot, are getting restless, and need exercise. So do you! Call the nearby parents and propose an afternoon outdoor snow bunny party. Youngsters to come in snowsuits, boots, mittens, caps, and other warm clothing. Mothers to bring a change of dry clothes.

Activities will depend on the ages, but almost every age likes to make snowmen. It can be a cooperative, big snowman, or a snowman contest—everybody making his own. Or try a miniature snowman contest with lots of foot-high snowmen or snow animals. If there's a safe hill or slope for sledding or sliding, provide dishpans, "flying saucers," pieces of heavy cardboard, or other material for sliding. If the play space is large enough, a snow fort with defenders and attackers will keep the slightly-olders busy and happy.

When mittens are soaked, snow is inside the boots, cheeks are bright red and noses and fingers cold, bring them indoors, change into dry clothes if necessary, and warm them up with hot soup, hot chocolate-with-a-marshmallow, and perhaps a hot dog in a toasted roll. Then the children go home with Mama or watch a TV show while you and the other mothers clear up the wet clothing, wash the dishes, and enjoy a cup of coffee. It's a nice change of pace for everyone, including housebound parents.

For the snow-shoveling, older children, give an invitation to bring their coworkers home for a warm-up. The same hot food, supplemented by table or floor games in the playroom, record-playing, or TV—all easy, friendly and informal. Don't forget to let the parents know where their youngsters are! They worry!

Water Baby Bash   vy

The nicest place to be on a hot, hot day is in or around water. The nicest thing to do is to get wet. The easiest sort of child play for water babies is water play.

* Think up as many ways to use water as possible. Collect or borrow such wonderful helps as lawn sprays, wading pools, washtubs of water, sprinkling cans, bottles, pails, tin or plastic cups, toy boats, other toys that float, soap-bubble mixture, pipes and other soap-bubble equipment for bubble-blowing (see below) , balloons.

* Telephone the mothers, tell about the party, invite them to a mother-child cooler. Children to wear swim suits or sun suits.

* Arrange deck chairs and serving tables for mothers where they can see and be responsible for their offspring.

* Serve a simple soup-and-sandwich lunch. Cool drinks for the grown-ups, milk for the children. Ice cream to make it a party.

* Set a time; 11 A.M. to 2 P.M. will cover the heat of the day and let the youngsters get their naps afterwards.

* Decide upon several informal activities. Sand play for the sandbox set (be sure the sand is moist) . Sprinkler run-throughs, if water shortage permits. Toy-floating and boat-sailing on the water in the big tub or in the wading pool. Balloon batting and

kicking. Bobbing for apples, if youngsters are old enough. General water play, such as pouring water in and out of containers, dipping, filling, and the like. Bubble-blowing as the Big Event. See Bubble Blow and Bubble Blow Pipes for how-to-do-its.

Bubble Blow

Collect one or more bowls, bubble pipes or rings, and substitutes such as spools, small funnels, soda straws. Cover the floor if used indoors.

To make: Rub a cake of yellow soap with your hands under warm water in a big bowl until the suds are heavy. Remove the suds with a big spoon. Test the water by blowing a bubble larger than your fist, dipping a finger into the bowl, then thrusting it into the bubble. If the bubble breaks, the solution is not strong enough. Rub in some more soap. A tablespoonful of sugar and two tablespoonfuls of glycerine will help make good strong bubbles. Add a bit of food coloring to make them prettier. These bubbles can be bounced, blown, poked and gently batted.

If the group is fairly small, they can all dip into one bowl. It works best to provide a larger group with several bowls, so that the youngsters play in smaller groups.

Bubble Blow Pipes

Provide a soda straw for each child. Make four tiny slits at one end of the straw and spread them out just a bit. That's the end to dip into the soapy water. Provide paper cups, the pointed-tip kind used in some dispensers. Clip the tips so that air can be blown through the cup. The wide rim will make a big bubble. Use small funnels the same way. Provide a supply of different sizes of spools.

To blow: Hold the bubble pipe or ring, the spool, paper cup, funnel or soda straw so that one end rests lightly on top of the soapy water. A film is all that's needed. Lift the pipe carefully, blow very gently through the dry end, and the bubble will start to form. When it is large enough, give a quick jerk to the pipe and the bubble will float free. Lovely!

No-Girls-Allowed Party   SO, AT

An all-boy party, birthday, camp-out, or whatever the occasion, requires *action*. The games can be a bit roughhouse, providing the boys are fairly evenly matched in age or weight. If not, handicap the older or heavier ones, or see that all dual contests are fairly matched. Games suitable for all-boy parties are often also suitable for use at camp, on the beach, on a hike, or other outdoor situations. Many should be modified if played indoors, unless the play area is a gym or large playroom.

Boys have great staying power. When the games are over and they have had a real he-man feed, a trip to the pool, beach, zoo or park might be a good addition. Or take them to a sports event, movie, or TV studio. Or send them off on a bike hike to one of the above, if the party is held in the daytime. (Night biking is *not* a good idea!)

Food for such an all-boy affair should be simple and plentiful. Set out a variety of spreads and fills, and let them make their own sandwiches. Provide a variety of cold soft drinks and hole-fillers like pretzels, pickles, peanuts, carrot sticks, popcorn, cheese crackers and such. If you have an outdoor grill, cook-your-own hot dogs or hamburgers can be substituted for sandwiches. Try to keep the eating period relaxed and long enough to give the boys a rest.

Get Dad to be on hand, and to lend a hand. For help in conducting some of the games, get a popular high school junior or senior to keep the gang moving but prevent mayhem.

Other themes for all-boy parties might be:

buccaneer island	he-men hike
camperee	bike-hike barbeque
stag party	beach boys' bash
hobo hole-up	clown circus
shipwreck party	cowboy round-up
pirate party	

Halloween Party   ALL

Halloween is the time of traditional trick-or-treat. Many communities plan special window-painting contests, and special evening parties, parades and other festivities for children, in an effort to get them off the streets and out of mischief. Find out about the plans of schools or other agencies. If not suitable, or too far away, plan a home Halloween party.

The home party that includes a trick-or-treat period is a good way to keep youngsters safe and happy, yet still feeling a part of one of the oldest of our special days. Safety, however, is a more important issue at Halloween than on any other holiday. Before going out to trick-or-treat, or to any outdoor party, parades or celebration, make sure that:

• The eyeholes of any mask are large enough for the child to see through them well.

• Masks of thin rubber are not used. They are dangerous to the child's breathing.

• Costumes are not long enough to get stepped on, and cause falls.

• Shoes are not too large or too high-heeled for running safely.

• No lighted candle is used in the jack-o'-lantern.

• The child carries a flashlight.

• The youngster does not enter any house where he does not know the people.

• The child does not accept any ride or invitations from strangers.

• No child goes off alone. The group should stay within stated neighborhood limits.

• No child goes home alone after the party.

A successful Halloween party needs the help of several adults and the agreement and understanding of the parents involved. Ask their help for special jobs:

• To accompany the group on the trick-or-treat mission (they stay in the background, but are there if needed. This is highly important with young children.)

• To supervise certain traditional party games, such as bob-bing for apples on a string, ducking for apples in a tub of water, telling a ghost story, and the like.

• To apply and to remove make-up before and after the trick-or-treat period. Provide lots of cold cream and grease paints. The children love it.

• To serve pre-trick-or-treat supper or refreshments (a good way to discourage the eating of too much candy and other treats).

• To take the children home after the party.

Decorations for the Halloween party are set by tradition. Lots of orange and black streamers, cut-outs of witches, black cats, skeletons, bats, and ghosts. Dim lights. Jack-o'-lanterns. Creepy music if you can find such records.

Favors are easy. Again they are expected to be traditional. Use items like trick-or-treat bags, lollipops with witch or jack-o'-lantern decorations, fortune cookies, mirrors, toy snakes, spiders, bugs, mice and other horrible make-believes, masks, apples, toy banks and the like.

Food, if eaten before going out on trick-or-treat, should be simple but substantial. A favorite hot dish, or fried chicken, mashed potatoes and gravy, milk, carrot sticks, celery, or other favorite dinner or supper food, including the ubiquitous ham-burgers. Simple dessert, perhaps a fruit jello. They'll have too many sweets later on.

Games should be adapted to the Halloween theme, and used to supplement the old favorites mentioned above. For the home Halloween party, especially for young and impressionable chil-dren, it is usually wise to omit the Chamber of Horrors type of program. Leave that for the larger school or community parties for the older youngsters.

Peanut Party   SO, AT

One of the easiest themes you can find, and always fun. Easily adapted to other symbols suitable for holiday parties. This sort of party works well with all-boys, all-girls, or with mixed groups. Activities suggested here can also be used for other parties. They work well with youngsters from seven to ten years of age. All you have to do is provide lots and lots of peanuts and plan ways to use them.

Invitations can be sheets of paper, decorated with a crayoned peanut or a real one glued on, rolled up and tied with colored string or ribbon. They might read something like this:

PEANUT PARTY—Please Come

> Where: In my yard
> When: Next Friday
> What time: 11 A.M. to 3 P.M.
> Signed: (child's name)
> P.S. Please don't dress up.

On the front door, place a large cut-out of a squirrel, or a stuffed-toy squirrel with a sign "Nut House." You and the party child can prepare in advance lots of peanuts with crayoned lines around their middles. They are for the peanut hunt; the different colors get different scores. A few should be wrapped in gold or silver foil for the top score, or for a special prize. Also have on hand supplies such as pipe cleaners, foil, paper, crayons, toothpicks, etc., for making peanut people or peanut animals; a jar for peanut dropping (see below), bags for carrying peanuts, and any other items that will be needed for the party. Activities can include:

• *Peanut treasure hunt.* Peanuts hidden all over the playing area, indoors or outdoors—*lots* of peanuts. Give everybody a bag, and set a time limit. Then count scores:

Gold peanut—10 points
Silver peanut—5 points
Red-line peanut—3 points
Blue-line peanut—2 points
Plain peanut—1 point

• *Peanut rolling.* The course should be about the length of a ping-pong table. Each youngster must roll a peanut with a toothpick (no pushing or tossing) from a starting to a finish line.

• *Peanut push* (for boys only). Same as above, but the peanut must be pushed by the nose only.

• *Peanut relays.* Each team member carries a peanut on the back of his hand, etc.

• *Peanut target.* Provide a dishpan, place a baking dish inside it, then place a wide-mouthed jar inside the baking dish. Each player tosses five peanuts. To score, those in the glass jar get five points; in the baking dish, three points; in the dishpan, one point.

• *Peanut pitching.* Contestants aim at a large target of paper or cardboard laid out on table or floor. Mark the target into many sections, the smaller the section, the higher the score it gets. Each player throws ten peanuts, then counts his score.

• *Peanut dropping.* Players drop peanuts into milk bottle or other container with a fairly large opening. The peanuts must be dropped from arm's length, no bending over.

• *Peanut shelling contest.* Messy but exciting.

• *Peanut creatures.* A contest to use peanuts to make all kinds of creatures: people, animals, birds, fish, etc. Hold an exhibit.

For food, use peanut butter, plus all sorts of sandwich makings, such as jelly, sliced tomatoes, strips of bacon, thin slices of apples, raisin bread, crackers, etc. Also serve lots of milk and ice cream.

Each child takes home all the peanuts he has won, plus a bag of peanut brittle, nut candy bars and the peanut creatures made. Then get out the vacuum cleaner if the party was indoors or the bamboo rake if the yard is full of peanut shells. They make good mulches if you have a garden.

Penny Party   SO, AT

A penny party is just as simple as the peanut party, and just as much fun. In fact, almost every game suggested for peanuts can be used just as well with pennies. Even the invitation can be similar with a bright, new penny glued to it:

PENNY PARTY—Please Come
This penny will buy your way into Bill Evans' party
Friday, September 10
Three to five-thirty, rain or shine

Decorate the front door with a cut-out of a big piggy bank. For favors, use small banks from the local novelty or five-and-dime stores, or perhaps the local bank. Bags of play money or candy coins should be on hand.

Almost all the games discussed under Peanut Party can be used, plus others in Chapters 8 and 9. Also see the Quick Party-planning Guide for games like Butterfingers, Blast Off and others at the slightly older and almost-teen age levels.

Bike Party   SO, AT

A bicycle is a major symbol for children, just as an automobile is for teen-agers. It is the child's first legitimate means of escape from home into personal independence. For those youngsters still under the magic spell of the bicycle, a Bike Party will be a wonderful theme. Easy as pie, too.

Invitations can be delivered by bike—with previous tele-phoned explanations to the parents, of course.

Bike Over to my House
Saturday, August 12, for a
BIKE PARTY
Five to Eight P.M.

Bicycle games take space. If you have a large yard or a tennis court, use them. If not, plan the party at a local park or play-ground. If you need a permit or special permission, be sure to get it ahead of time. In any event, plan to meet at the home of the young host or hostess.

To start the party off on the right wheels, decorate. Provide strips of crepe paper in lots of different colors. Each guest decorates his own bike. Then have a bicycle parade around the yard or other party area, or around the block. Hold contests when all children are back and ready for action.

• *Shoe scramble.* This can be for boys vs. boys, girls vs. girls, or girls vs. boys. Players place their shoes, *not* tied together, in a pile in the center of the playing area. Then each team goes to the opposite end and lines up. At the signal, they ride their bikes up to within ten feet of the pile of shoes. Each must then dismount, find his shoes, put them on, and then ride his bike back to his starting line. First team to all get back wins. Play best out of three tries.

• *Coasting.* Each rider pedals hard for fifteen feet, then coasts. Mark the spot where each stops. Rider whose bike coasts farthest wins.

• *Snails.* You'll have to lay out a course about fifty to a hundred feet long, if possible, with lanes from three to six feet wide. A tennis court makes a good course. At the signal, the riders go as slowly as possible. They must not touch a foot to the ground, or get out of a lane, or turn around. Anyone who does is OUT. The last rider to cross the finish line is the winner.

• *Wet heads.* Each rider must take a paper cup full of water, hold it over the top of his head with one hand, and race his bike to a finish line. The winning player out of the first two to get back is the one with the most water left in his cup.

• *Blind race.* Mark off a very short finish line, not more than twenty-five feet away. Each player races separately in this contest, so there is no danger of collision. He lines up at the starting line, is blindfolded, then rides until he *thinks* his rear wheel is on the finish line. The best guesser wins. Try two out of three.

• *Slalom race.* Set up chairs, boxes, or other hazards along the course, making it wind in and around the objects. Each rider races through the course. Time him with a stopwatch. No one may touch an object, put a foot to the ground, or miss going by or around the hazards. Run this race in heats if necessary.

After the bike contests, hold some of the tapering off games (see Chapter 9) before eating. A cook-out, with lots of mixings for sandwiches, salads, and fancy drinks makes a good ending for such an active party.

Trike Party   VY

Just like the bike party, but planned for the tricycle set. Make the distances shorter, and add a few straight races and relays, if necessary.

You can add novelty to the trike party by inviting the boys and girls to wear their cowboy or cowgirl costumes. Then give a Western twist by changing the names of the games to suit the theme, such as Round-up for the Shoe Scramble, Water-Hole Race for Wet Heads, etc.

Other possible names for bike and trike parties:

> pedal-pushing party
> two-wheel spin party
> handlebar hoedown
> wheeler-dealer party

Trip Party   ALL

This type of party is especially good when the home area is limited or not suited for the play activities of a number of children, or when you don't feel equal to conducting a game program, or when it will be fun to go somewhere.

The first job you will have to do is to decide how, how many, and where. How will the guests travel—by family car, station wagon, bus, train, bicycle or by walking? The method of transportation will affect the number of guests and the kinds of activities possible en route. Whatever the method, however, a responsible adult or older teen-ager should be provided for every eight of the Slightly Olders and the Almost-Teens, and for every three or four of the Very Youngs.

It is a good idea, when traveling by car, to be well-supplied with paper towels, and to check ahead of time on the rest rooms of the service stations along the route. Some child will probably become car sick, especially if the trip is in the winter and the car windows are shut. And when one child needs a bathroom, they all will!

It is also a good idea to give each youngster some sort of identification. It can be party-pretty, such as a lei, cowboy neckerchief, bright armband, or a big, bright badge, but it should be large enough and bright enough to be seen easily.

In a car or bus, the youngsters should stay in their seats (seat-belted in, if possible). Since movement is restricted, singing and quiet games of words and observation can be used to make the trip pleasant.

Games make the trip shorter, and can be played by seat partners or by those along the two sides of the car or bus. Alphabet is a simple game. Each child takes turns in trying to see some object starting with each letter of the alphabet: A for auto, alfalfa, aster, aqueduct; B for boy, bicycle, bus; C for cow, cat, crow, etc. Colors is a similar type of game. One child or group on one side of the car or bus takes one color, such as red. The seatmate or the group on the other side might take blue. Each keeps count of the number of objects of that color that they see. The largest number wins. Other games possible, with perhaps minor changes, are Crazy Answers, Snip, Shopping, Foo and Koo, Bumble Bee Buzz, Catch a Smile, and Simon Says (see Quick Party-planning Guide).

The length of the trip and the trip party should be based on the age levels of the children; the younger they are, the shorter the trip and the party.

If the trip party goes to a park or playground, bring along whatever simple equipment you may need for active games. Balloons, several balls, and a supply of peanuts or pennies will be enough to let you use many of the games in Chapter 8.

Possible trip objectives might include:

- A movie, chosen for child appeal
- A puppet show
- Planetarium (check on the show schedule)

- Museum of natural history (select special sections to suit the age level and to prevent fatigue)
  - Young folks' concert or ballet (get tickets in advance)

If you plan to eat out, often a very special treat for children, select a place that will be a novelty, but not too exotic in its food. Children are often very conservative in their food likes and dislikes, and will cling to the known. Schoolchildren may be familiar with a cafeteria if their school has one, but all children are enthralled with the Automat. Trying to use chopsticks in a Chinese or Japanese restaurant is often fun, too. Or if the weather is good, you might take a box lunch for each child, and eat in a park or playground.

Whatever you do, and wherever you go—don't stay too long. Trips are tiring, even for the Almost-Teens. Get them all back home when you said you would. And don't forget a party favor or souvenir. It won't be a real party without one.

Balloon Bango Party   ALL

Probably nothing but the ice cream cone rivals the balloon in child popularity. Probably no other party asset is as colorful, inexpensive, versatile and easy to find. A balloon party can fit almost any occasion, and balloon activities can be used in many other theme parties (see Circus Party) .

For a balloon party, use all sorts of balloons: the small, fat ones; the long, sausage-shaped ones; the big ones, and the kind that blow up into clown and animal shapes. If the party is indoors, decorate the ceiling. Inflate lots of balloons, tie them securely, rub them for several seconds on your wool skirt or slacks, and the static electricity generated will make them bounce up to the ceiling and stay there! Pretty!

Games and play activities can include Balloon Birds, Jet Rocket, Chopstick Relay, Kangaroo Hop, and Kick Up (see Quick Party-planning Guide) . Add others, such as Balloon Relay, that involves the passing of a balloon up and down a team's line;

Balloon Kick, in which youngsters must kick a balloon across a finish line and back; Balloon Break (not for the Very Youngs), in which each player ties his balloon to his belt or his ankle, then tries to break those of other players while protecting his own. Balloon Bat, played like a simple volleyball game in which two teams bat a balloon back and forth across a net or rope, each team scoring a point when the other team lets the balloon touch the ground, is another good game for the Slightly Olders. Or use balloons instead of potatoes in the old favorite, the potato race. Butt the Balloon is great fun, too, using the head only, no hands or feet. If balloon games give out, or if the youngsters begin to lose interest, switch to some of the penny or peanut games. They combine well with balloon activities.

Food can be carnival-like: hot dogs with all the fixings, ice cream cones, spun-sugar candy if you can find it, chocolate milk, pink lemonade.

Favors can include those wonderful, big, special balloons that have pebbles or other noisemakers inside, balloons on sticks, balloons with the children's names painted on them. Small game equipment, such as jacks, tops, marbles, kites, and jumpropes make nice favors for spring or early summer parties.

Books and Pamphlets with More Help

Enjoy Your Child—Ages 1, 2 and 3, by J. L. Hymes, Jr. Public Affairs Pamphlet # 141, 381 Park Ave., S., New York, N.Y. 10016.

Handbook for Recreation, Children's Bureau Publication # 231, revised, 1959, by Virginia Musselman, available from Superintendent of Documents, Government Printing Office, Washington, D.C. 20004.

Instant Picnic Fun, by Virginia Musselman, published by Association Press, 291 Broadway, New York, N.Y. 10007.

Junior Party Book, The, by Bernice Wells Carlson, published by Abingdon Press, Nashville, Tenn. 37202.

Parent's Guide to Children's Play and Recreation, by Alvin Schwartz, published by P. F. Collier, Inc., 866 Third Ave., New York, N.Y. 10022.

Party Book for Boys and Girls, The, by Bernice Wells Carlson, published by Abingdon Press, Nashville, Tenn. 37202.

Play Activities for Boys and Girls, by Richard Kraus, published by McGraw-Hill Book Co., Inc., New York, N.Y. 10036.

Play for Preschoolers, prepared by the Physical Fitness Division of the Department of National Health and Welfare, Ottawa, Canada.

Singing Games, by Muriel McGann, available from the National Recreation and Park Association, 1700 Pennsylvania Ave., N.W., Washington, D.C. 20006.

Your Child from One to Six and *Your Child from Six to Twelve,* both Children's Bureau publications, available from Superintendent of Documents, Government Printing Office, Washington, D.C. 20004.

This book may be kept

FOURTEEN DAYS

A fine of TWO CENTS will be charged for each day
the book is kept over time.

Feb 12 '51			
Apr 14 '55			
ay 4 '56			
Mar 20 '57			
Apr 30 '57			
Jul 13 '64			
Feb 1 '72			
Mar 3 '75			
Mar 17 '75			